BALLET CLASS

1 Lines of dance

BALLET CLASS

Principles and Practice

JOAN LAWSON

with photographs by
Ross MacGibbon

Adam & Charles Black, London • Theatre Arts Books, New York

First published 1984
by A & C Black (Publishers) Limited
35 Bedford Row, London WC1R 4JH

Published simultaneously in USA
by Theatre Arts Books
153 Waverly Place, New York, NY 10014

UK ISBN 0-7136-2416-7
US ISBN 0-87830-164-X

Lawson, Joan
    Ballet class.
    1. Ballet—Study and teaching
    I. Title   II. MacGibbon, Ross
    792.8′ 2′ 07   GV1788.5

    ISBN 0-7136-2416-7

Printed in Great Britain by The Whitefriars Press Limited, London, Tonbridge and
Chichester.

Contents

Photographs

Preface – a personal statement

This book has been written at the request of my many friends in the world of dance and ballet. It is an attempt to summarise all I have written on the theory of technique in my other books. But it is different in that I am trying to explain how I put theory into practice. During my tours of England, the United States and Australia I have often been asked to write down my exercises through which I discuss and demonstrate how I teach certain exercises and why I concentrate on the Seven Principles of Classical Dance instead of some syllabus.

Such a task is somewhat daunting because an exercise meant for one class may have to be adapted for particular students or situations. Nevertheless I hope what is given herein will be of value. Although the sets of eighteen classes have been worked out in detail to cover an Elementary, Intermediate and Advanced class for six of the Principles of Classical Dance – Stance, Turn-out, Placing, Laws of Balance, Transfer of Weight and the Rules – there are no classes for the seventh and most important Principle: Co-ordination. (See *photo 1*.)

The classes follow the usual pattern and order of most schools. Each exercise also involves several other principles because it is impossible to isolate one from the others and expect a line of dance to emerge. Nevertheless, when explaining my ways of teaching I have always tried to concentrate on one principle only during a single class in order to draw attention to the part it must play in all dance movements. In this way the most important Principle – Co-ordination – has been covered. Without it there can be no feeling for the line of dance drawn by the performer's whole body to fill the space in which it moves, nor will the performer reveal how the movements are phrased to cover the whole stage and timed to become one with the music.

The classes are intended to help all those involved in classical dance, particularly those who, having had a professional career, now hope to become teachers and, secondly, those students in training colleges with no professional experience. These two kinds of prospective teacher naturally have to approach their task differently. It is perhaps appropriate that I should try and explain why I concentrate on the Principles before offering advice on what to do to become a teacher. These were items I had to work out for myself when I left the stage to become a critic. Then when I left criticism to go the other side of the curtain and become a teacher. And finally when I had to teach aspiring as well as experienced teachers.

CONCENTRATING ON THE PRINCIPLES

It was when researching into the history of ballet that I became absorbed in John Weaver. His *Anatomical and Mechanical Lectures on Dancing* (1723) gave a clear analysis of how the actions of bones, ligaments, tendons and muscles related to dance. This first introduction to anatomy urged me to continue the study. When Dame Ninette de Valois invited me to give some lectures on how to develop a strong back and correct breathing, which were the hallmark of the Russian school (my own background), I sought help from the late Professor Wiles of Middlesex Hospital. Although knowing little about classical dance, his quick eyes and confident hand or finger drawing lines on my body made me realise that the first need was to study the bone structure. Without that knowledge I could not fully understand why I held myself differently when taking classical stance. Moreover, if the many bones of spine and legs were not fully stretched and balanced one over the other, guided upwards by the head, I could not hold turn-out.

This brought into question the functions of the ball and socket joints at hip level and, later, all the other different types of joint that activate the arms, knees, elbows and so on. When I asked what happened when I moved my limbs and torso in different ways, if only to stand in one of the five positions of feet and arms, the Professor went on to describe the various groups of muscles. He made me note carefully how they helped me to move freely because throughout the body they had been specially educated to counter-balance each other. This meant that I could balance easily from one position to another as in a *grand rond de jambe* or transfer weight from one leg to another in a *grand jeté en avant*.

It was Professor Wiles' profound knowledge of the breathing apparatus (he was an ear, nose and throat specialist) that helped me when I first attempted to analyse the breathing needed during a solo in order not to finish breathless. This had never been a problem because I probably did it instinctively. Nevertheless it was a revelation when he explained that I took breath in order to give extra impetus to a *pirouette* or jump, how I 'topped up' during a series of *changements* and how I 'puffed out' quickly before setting off and taking in another breath for another jump, or how I 'held it' and exhaled very slowly when sustaining a pose. Above all he made me understand a dancer's need to learn to phrase movement as a singer phrases a song.

It was when listening to Dame Ninette teaching that I realised the utmost importance of the Principles listed above, viz. Stance, Turn-out, Placing, Laws of Balance, Transfer of Weight and Rules. I decided to tabulate her Rules and began to work out classes based on the six Principles. I decided to teach one Principle throughout one class whilst still using the form and order of any normal syllabus. This meant considering every exercise and what to add or subtract to achieve my purpose. It was Dame Ninette's insistence on the exact placing and/or height of the working leg that gave me the most important clue to all types of *battement*; her demands for the most economical and therefore simplest ways of moving from one step or pose to another by accurate changes of weight, balance or direction, sometimes made by the whole body, that helped me to formulate my ideas for all types of *ronds de jambe* and rotations; and, even more important, her advice on the shape, length and breadth of the lines to be drawn in any kind of step that helped me to decide how best to give quality and the right impetus to one or another part of the body and life to the simplest exercise in the centre after having made preparatory explorations during *barre*-work.

My preparatory exercises at the *barre* were also designed to help students discover their own capacity for movement and use that to the fullest extent. At the same time however they had to adhere to the Principles. This was particularly important in all types of *battements tendus* where the student should be trying to establish the size of step needed. This can range from a mere parting of the feet from 5th to 4th for a *relevé échappé* or *pirouette en dehors* to the largest lunge into a *grand port de bras*. In the same way, the exact height of the raised leg in a *battement glissé* is important. This can decide the length of a *glissade*, the height of a *jeté* and even the whip-lash movement of the working leg which sends a dancer round in *pirouette fouettée en tournant en dedans*.

Between visits to the School named Vaganova (Leningrad) and the Moscow Choreographic Academy I clarified my ideas on developing a balanced class able to produce dancers capable of meeting the challenge of a varied repertoire. They had to adapt their bodies to the lyricism of Fokine and Ashton, the bravura of Petipa and the complexity of MacMillan as well as the characterisation demanded by Massine, Robbins and others. However it was not until I visited the Royal Danish Ballet as a critic and sat as a guest watching classes in Bournonville methods that I grasped the value of rapidly changing *épaulements*. This led to my use of exercises at the *barre* and in the centre where quick changes of weight, *épaulement* and direction helped students to develop their sense of balance, speed and accuracy. I found it particularly helpful for those having difficulty in centring their weight firmly on one leg and then making the very slight transfer to the other. Once they could manage this, it became easier for them to make the difficult transition when the

body has to make a half-turn without displacing the hips during *fouettés relevés* or *sautés*, and *grands jetés en tournant*.

Finally, it was Dame Ninette's insistence on the need *consciously* to co-ordinate the movements of the whole body to create a line of dance that made me understand the need for every dancer, no matter of what age or standard, to control every movement. At the same time, the movements had always to be economical and simple.

As we all know, the devlopment of dance is a continuing process. From the simple folk dance, it became the pastime of Louis XIV's courtiers and the career of the first professionals. The art spread to Russia, Austria, Scandinavia, back to France and Denmark, back to Russia, to England and so on, a little like my own journeying. Having started with folk dance, the step to Margaret Morris' Greek dance was easy for she had a sound knowledge of anatomy and classical dance, particularly placing. It was this which took me to Russia to which I have continually returned. France and Denmark have also played a large part in my thinking and if Italy appears to have played little part, it is because my Russian colleagues and above all Dame Ninette's profound understanding of the pertinent parts of Cecchetti's own teaching have seen to it that the Italian influence rubbed off on me.

I have thought it best to divide the book into three sections. Firstly, Advice to Teachers, so that they are encouraged to use their eyes and ears as well as their bodies when standing up in front of a class. Secondly, the Classes where I preface each section with advice on what to look for when assessing students in movement. Thirdly, because I have so often had to help injured dancers back to work, I give Remedial Work. This begins with so-called 'Flat Barre', which is prefaced by some words of advice. There follow Floor Exercises, which have proved beneficial to the more seriously injured. These used to be given as soon as possible after an injury or operation but, under surgeon's orders, they are sometimes given beforehand to keep muscles in tone. Some of the Floor Exercises have also helped students with physical problems of Stance, Turn-out and Placing and have been introduced to general classes. Finally in the third section, I have included a few remarks on particular injuries which require specialised treatment.

The photographs, specially taken by Ross MacGibbon of The Royal Ballet, are of two kinds. Those illustrating Advice to Teachers are of scholars of The Royal Academy of Dancing, by kind premission of the late Alan Hooper, its Director. They show various details and the Focal Points upon which teachers should concentrate during the early stages of training. Those illustrating the classes are of many friends in The Royal Ballet, who agreed to help and who, incidentally, are largely responsible for all my efforts as teacher and writer. Their photos attempt to show how this or another step or pose can look very different when danced on the stage, although the principle involved remains the same. As costumes can change the look of the dance, I asked my dancers to perform in their usual practice tights so that their lines of movement are clearly defined.

It is to those dancers that I must give my most grateful thanks: Michael Batchelor, Stephen Beagley, Bryony Brind, Phillip Broomhead, Fiona Chadwick, Nicholas Dixon, Anthony Dowson, Sharon McGorian, Ashley Page, Karen Paisey, David Peden, Julie Rose, Stephen Sherriff and Ravenna Tucker. To spare so much time during one of their busiest seasons is evidence of their generosity and love of their art. I must also thank most profoundly the thoughtfulness of David Wall, Alfreda Thoroughgood and Stuart Beckett for going through my script and classes. Without their expertise and knowledge of movement I might never have put on paper what they know to be part of dance.

Joan Lawson

PART ONE
Advice to Teachers

To the Professional Dancer

The transition from stage to class-room is not easy. To dance on the stage is not to dance in the class-room. A professional career teaches dancers how to project personality and to give themselves generously to an audience across the large gap between the stage and the back of the gallery. But in this reaching-out beyond the footlights, much of the class-room discipline is lost. Choreographers work in various styles and in different ways, and because they are creators and not teachers not all of them exercise the same strict discipline. It is easy, therefore, for many dancers to lose sight of the principles upon which their own technique is based.

Before they can satisfactorily pass on their knowledge to others, they must refresh their memories and retrain their own bodies so that they know how and why the first exercises should be performed. As teachers, they are in intimate contact with their pupils. Whereas some exaggeration may be desirable in front of an audience to show off a *pirouette* or to express emotion or mood in the line of dance, anything of the kind must be suppressed in the class-room. The younger the pupils, the more necessary it is to give a calmly disciplined demonstration.

The dancer must now take an objective view of a movement and not a subjective one. For example: if a dancer, in 2nd position of the feet and arms, spreads the arms wide above shoulder level to express the energy and exhilaration of leaping up in a *grand échappé* before a group of 8 to 10 year olds, the children may well attempt – and succeed – in doing likewise, the result being raised shoulders and tensed neck as they land, with heels NOT down on the floor as they should be.

To the Dance Student

Dance students without professional experience are handicapped in a different way. Because they have not had to learn how to give out to an audience, they are less aware than the professional dancer of the need to draw a line in space. Too often their training involves only the ability to memorise a series of exercises and to repeat them endlessly, while the purpose is forgotten. Such students have learnt to place themselves, often correctly, in each pose and position, but not to draw a line from one placing to the next. This leads to a purely mechanical approach. In other words, they do not dance.

Abrupt and often angular transitions from one step to another happen when the students forget one or other of the Rules. This may be that neither arms nor legs should overcross the centre line of the body, or that the head should always lead the movement.

A different amalgamation of steps, or a slight change in a *port de bras* may find students at a loss. This is particularly noticeable when they are faced with the many variations on the *temps lié*. In all of them the pattern of the footwork remains the same, danced diagonally forwards (or backwards) and then directly sideways. But the sequence can start with a *pirouette*, a *sissonne ordinaire* into a *chassé assemblé porté*, or a *tour en l'air*. The *ports de bras* can remain the same, or they can be immensely varied. (See *temps lié*, pages 49, 53, 67, 77, 79, 90, 105.)

To All Teachers

It is not enough to study the many syllabi laid down by different organisations. For the good teacher, these are only a basis, the first step in a continuing process. Each item in a sequence should be valued as a segment of the whole vocabulary of dance. It does not form part of only one given sequence but can and will be related to other steps and poses. It can be retimed, made more or less important, given different alignments, *épaulements* or *ports de bras*. Yet whatever the context, the basic principles of classical dance must at all costs be maintained.

Teachers must train their eyes and ears as well as their bodies if they are to help their students to be both technically and musically co-ordinated. When Fokine had newly become a teacher and was experimenting with his students, he laid particular emphasis on the exact matching of step and pose to musical note and phrase, in order to convey a visual impression of the music, as he did later in *Les Sylphides* (see photo 2). He remarked that the dancer must 'go to, through and from the note'. His students had to time every detail of an *enchaînement* for the sake of its classical line and purely technical form. Fokine's eyes saw any mistake immediately: legs and arms that did not unfold simultaneously in a *battement fondu*, a less than exact placing and timing of a series of *ronds de jambe à terre* as his students turned themselves and paused momentarily at each corner of the studio in *pointe tendue*.

Understanding the Body

I said earlier that professional dancers who wish to be teachers must retrain their bodies and must learn how and why exercises should be performed. For this purpose, and to understand the different physiques which teachers have to deal with, they must acquire some knowledge of anatomy and the muscular co-ordination of bones, ligaments, tendons and joints in order to draw smooth lines of dance. And they should also understand the role of the brain in prompting muscular activity.

This anatomical study must be related to the principles of classical dance. These relationships are, briefly, as follows:

A Stance requires knowledge of the spine from head to coccyx, of the articulation of the vertebrae, one with another, and of the muscles which give the spine mobility and help with breathing.

B Turn-out requires an understanding of the ball-and-socket joints of the hips and of the ligaments and muscles which activate the legs. A somewhat similar study is needed of the ball-and-socket joints of the shoulders and of the muscles within the thighs, pelvis, stomach and torso.

C Placing requires a knowledge of other joints (varying in type) and their relationship to the bones as well as of the parts of a limb and their relationship to each other and to the whole.

D Laws of balance require a study of all groups of muscles, of how they counteract with each other and of how dancers must continually centre their weight, always directing their movement by the head, the heaviest part of the body.

E Transfer of weight can be understood only by a combined examination of all the above studies. Only then is it possible to ensure correct adjustments for the control of muscles and thus to enable dancers to hold or pass through any type of pose or step to another.

F Rules. If a proper anatomical study has been made covering the points listed above, it should become evident why John Weaver began to lay down basic rules in 1723, to which later masters have added many more – to all of which teachers should adhere. If they are strictly followed, technical faults will be quickly spotted by a teacher who can correct a class in general terms – and then help a particular student in difficulty.

2   A visual impression of the music

Drawing Lines of Dance

A dancer can draw only three types of line with the body. These can be straight, rounded or angled and in every dance movement they are used simultaneously. Correct Stance requires the spine and legs to be straight, but an angle at the feet. If the arms are relaxed or in *bras bas*, they are rounded. In *ronds de jambe*, the lines are more complex. The legs are straight, but the working one is at an angle to the supporting leg and is propelled round by the action of many muscles. Another example is the subtle straightening of the elbow alone when one arm falls from a rounded position in 5th to an *arabesque*, whilst the other circles downwards behind its own shoulder. This lowering of the arms requires careful adjustment of the bones in their sockets if the shoulders are not to lose their alignment (see photos 3a, b, c).

In some of my exercises I have found it invaluable to feel with my own body how to draw lines, particularly straight and curved lines. I then know better how to press a hand or just a finger on students straight up the length of the spine, or down from the waist, up the side of the torso from hip to armpit, across the back or front of shoulders or chest, or down the centre of leg or foot, and so on, indicating the direction in which the students should stretch and/or relax – though their muscles are sometimes reluctant to respond. This seems to help some students, particularly when they are in full growth or injured in some way.

It is only by feeling the line to be drawn that dancers learn to understand the subtle changes in their movements created by such choreographers as Ashton and MacMillan. The most obvious example is the change from the turned-in leg and arm of the famous statue of Mercury to the classical *attitude* established by Blasis. (See photos 37a, b, page 70.) Another is the change from a true *arabesque penchée* with its straight line from extended toe to head, which requires a full stretch of the spine and perfect control over balance, to the *arabesque allongée* with its more gently stretched curving line over a supporting leg *en fondu*.(See photo 33, page 58, and photo 40, page 74.)

a

b   *c*

3 Lines of dance in Robbins' *Afternoon of a Faun* (Ashley Page):
a Angles; *b* Curves; *c* Several lines

Training the Eyes

The work of the eyes in spotting a fault should be obvious to every teacher. But it is often difficult to ascertain whether the fault is due to misunderstanding, to poor technique, or to some physical problem. The teacher's own experience of feeling a particular movement with his or her body should reveal which Rule is being broken. But if the fault does not respond to correction, the teacher's eyes must look more closely at the student's physique in order to solve the problem.

1   The Hip Line: 'Stand straight' (see photo 4)
The first and possibly most important focal point is the whole pelvic area, particularly the hip line. The student adopts correct Stance – or is it? Is the hip line level? Does it lie parallel to the floor? And to the shoulders? If the answer is NO, then it is possible that the legs are not equally turned out and that there is a slight twist of the pelvis to remedy matters. This can cause a variety of faults. For example: there may be a slight twist to the left so that the right knee then twists inwards and is not directly over the middle of the right foot and directly under the right hip; or the foot may roll inwards or sickle outwards; or the right side of the torso may be sunk into the right hip; the toes of both feet may be clenched to maintain balance because the weight is not evenly centred over both legs. As one fault may give rise to endless others, it is important to find the main cause of the trouble before attempting to correct the fault first spotted.

2   Feet: 'Are you standing comfortably?' (see photos 5a and b)
Perhaps the second important point is to observe the response to the question, 'Are you standing comfortably?' This can be a good opening to a class because the way a child stands on two feet can make or mar the first steps in classical dance. If the position is not comfortable, there is little chance of obtaining correct Stance.

The teacher must first ensure that the feet are placed firmly on the floor with the weight equally distributed over the three points of balance: the centre of balance should be directly over the middle of the longitudinal arch (that is a point between the heel and the big and little toe joints, i.e. the metatarsal arch).

If the child then rises on one *demi-pointe*, he or she should be able to sense a pressure point somewhere between the first and second toes at metatarsal level. If this is so, the foot will not roll inwards or sickle outwards, the ankle will be centred directly over the longitudinal arch and under the knee, and a line drawn upwards would run through the centre of the body.

With some children this may not be possible because of their natural shape and the way their bones are put together. For example: if there is any form of bowing

4

5a

5b

4   The hip line
5   The legs: *a* turned in; *b* turned out

5

either in the lower leg or at knee level, or sway-back (hyper-extended) legs; if the feet are set at a slight angle to the legs and appear naturally to sickle inwards or outwards. In such cases it is possible with time and patience to re-educate the muscles and thus straighten the look of the leg line – but this can only be done if the rest of the body, particularly the muscles in the thighs and pelvic region, are capable of re-education so that they can control and activate the legs and/or feet in their new alignment.

3 The Upper Torso: 'Keep those shoulders down!' (see photo 6)

The third point to assess is the torso, particularly the area between the waist and head. If the spine shows any resistance when a hand is drawn firmly upwards in a straight line and does not respond easily to a slight touch to curve it forwards above the waist, there may be several reasons. Firstly, the 'tail' has not been pulled downwards to the heels. Secondly, tension has been caused by the shoulders and arms being pressed too far backwards so that the shoulder-blades rest on the rib-cage and the chest has been raised too far upwards. Thirdly, the head has not been held properly, so that the spine is arched and tense. If the legs are now opened into 2nd position, it will be seen that the weight is held too far back on the heels.

Alternatively the 'tail' may have been 'tucked under' and the shoulders pressed towards each other in the hope of achieving a better Turn-out. In the effort to straighten the spine there is now a greater degree of arching and tension because the weight has been pressed even further backwards. This can be highly damaging to groin and knees if the habit persists.

4 The Legs: 'Pull up those knees!'

The fourth important focal point must be the legs and particularly their action as they turn outwards in the hip-joints. It may happen, as noted above (1), that the legs are not equally turned out from the hip-joints or one leg may be longer than the other. The student should be encouraged to turn out or stretch equally, so that both knees remain centred and well straightened when the feet are in any of the five positions. This may mean that the feet in 5th are not very tightly closed together, but at least there will be no twisting of the knees, pelvis or feet. It will also mean that when a leg is raised at any height to the side, the leg will not be directly at the side even though the angle between the raised and supporting legs will appear correct. It is not a good idea to throw the raised leg up and over backwards as students try to do – this can only cause hip and torso problems on the supporting side.

The point of difficulty for students with such a problem is in *grands ronds de jambe*. Particular notice must be taken of how they circle the leg from side to back and vice-versa. Weight must be seen to be firmly centred over the supporting leg, with the torso pulled upwards. As soon as the leg begins to circle from side to back, the dancer must simultaneously tilt the pelvis slightly forwards and stretch the upper torso backwards, leading with the head. For movement *en dedans*, the pelvis and upper torso must simultaneously stretch upwards just after the leg leaves *arabesque*. At the start of these two movements, students must never move outwards from the perpendicular line of the supporting leg. And there must be no sinking into the supporting side or any displacement of the hips.

The same displacement often takes place in students who do have equal Turn-out, and must be corrected. Otherwise it will affect particularly any rotation or *fouetté*. For these movements it is absolutely essential that the working leg is fully stretched in front or behind, the raised toe in a direct line with the supporting heel.

The student should be reminded that it is by turning the supporting leg, and NOT the raised leg, that the hips, and the whole pelvic area, can be adjusted.

6 Upper torso

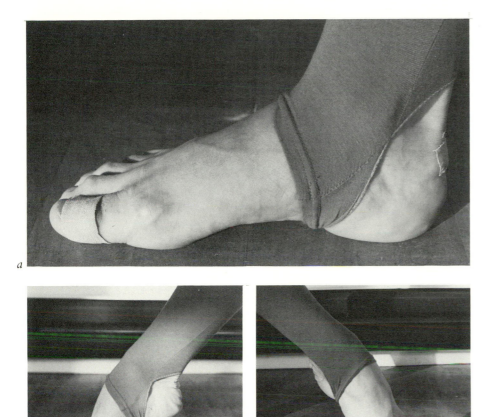

7 The action of the feet (Sharon McGorian)
a foot flat on floor; *b* correctly pointed toe; *c* incorrectly pointed foot with toes clenched

5 The Action of Feet and Legs: 'Stretch those feet!'

The fifth focal point is the exact relationship and Placing of the feet and knees. Much time must be spent on these for they will be so much affected by individual structure. Ideally the knees should be directly over the centre of the foot, whether they are bent or straight, turned in or out. The feet, when placed in any of the five positions should be at right angles to the perpendicular legs. The three points of balance remain the big and little toe joints and the heel. If balance is not correctly centred over these three points, the teacher must help to re-educate the various muscles in order to achieve it. This requires patience for there are so many muscles involved, even more when the student has to maintain balance over one leg.

The student then has to set the weight over the three points without twisting the supporting hip, lifting the working hip, twisting the shoulders or sinking into the hips in some way. This can be helped if the teacher insists that the student practises rising straight up and down on *demi-pointe* (no higher) along a perpendicular line without bending that knee, so that the centre is always stable. The working leg should be held firmly in a low *retiré*.

To achieve the correct movement for this exercise and for *battements tendus*, concentrate on the action of the foot moving outwards and inwards from one of the closed positions to *pointe tendue*. As the foot moves outwards, weight fully on the supporting leg, the ankle must immediately begin to stretch. Then, as soon as the pads of the toes begin to leave the floor, the metatarsal bones must be drawn together, the toes stretched downwards to their tips (not downwards or clenched under) and the heel must not be pulled backwards into the Achilles tendon. On returning inwards from the fully stretched leg, the toes should be held as the ankle gradually relaxes. Just before the heel begins to touch the floor, the metatarsal arch and toes should also gradually relax in preparation for sharing weight equally with the supporting leg when the working foot is drawn up tightly, knees fully stretched. (See photos 7a; b and c.)

At this point the weight of the upper body must be held firmly away from the hips. There is a danger that the dancer may continually press the metatarsal arch on the floor on the return journey, so that the toes curl upwards. As a result, the movement does not flow evenly through the whole leg and the weight is wrongly centred. Moreover, the toes have lost contact with the floor at that very point when, in a jump or *relevé*, they must give the final impetus to send the body upwards and to guide the leg or legs correctly downwards on the return. I believe that if such pressure on the metatarsal arch is allowed, it may lead to the many stress fractures now prevalent. For the dancer is likely to land with the weight too far back and, in an attempt to sustain balance, to lift the heel off the floor. This only results in the toes being clenched and in some cases the spine as well, for its natural curves, if tense, cannot resist the shock of landing. (See photo 8.)

Whenever the foot is working properly – which is particularly apparent when it is raised in *retiré* before the leg unfolds in a *développé* and closes *sur le cou de pied* before *petits battements* – the shaping of it should look elegant and it should not sickle outwards. Such sickling may look pretty but it can be highly dangerous when practised by students whose Turn-out is not one hundred per cent correct.

An important Rule to stress at all times is: the tips of the toes should never leave the floor in any simple exercise commencing with *battement tendu*, but once off the floor, they must remain fully stretched until they touch it on return, no matter how high the leg rises. It is, therefore, most important to cultivate the correct action of the foot and ankle described above. Students must understand how to bend the foot downwards and upwards to an angle of 90° or more at the ankle joint without curling the toes in any way while they work the muscles in the metatarsal arch.

Another important Rule to stress is the need to press the heels immediately into and out of the floor from a *demi-plié* if height is to be gained in any type of jump or if a *relevé* is to have absolute stability.

6 The Arms: 'Round those elbows!' (see photo 9)

A sixth point to note is how the arms are set in their sockets and their shape. The ideal arms are those which round easily when held *bras bas*, then raised upwards through 1st position to 5th and then opened to 2nd before being lowered to *bras bas*, making a perfect circle without any apparent movement of the shoulder-blades. The arms should rotate independently in their sockets and never fall behind the shoulder line.

The hyper-extended arm, like the hyper-extended leg (the so-called sway-back) requires remedial guidance. Pupils with this problem should be taught never to use their fullest stretch when moving the arm into *arabesque* position, in order to maintain the necessary straight line unbroken. Instead, they must learn to FEEL when the arm looks straight and is not tensed or stretched forwards from the shoulder. (In the same way, those with sway-back legs must learn to FEEL and SEE that the supporting leg is absolutely perpendicular and that the knee is pulled upwards by both inner and outer thigh muscles and NOT backwards, which is how they feel that the knee should be stretched.) Such types of arm and leg require much re-education of the muscles.

8   Jumping feet – at these ages not always fully stretched
9   The arms are always rounded except in *arabesque*

10   The differences between boys and girls – compare shoulder and arm lines: *a bras bas*; *b* second and fifth positions

Ideally both boys and girls should possess arms which allow the insides of the hands and elbows to face front when in 2nd position, the body when in 1st and the head when in 5th. If this is not naturally present, small adjustments can be made by rotating the upper arms slightly in their sockets. If they appear to hang slightly forwards when in 2nd position, they should be rotated backwards (as legs are turned outwards). Or if they hang too far back with dropped elbows, then rotated slightly inwards. They must never be lifted over or appear as if hung from above because the upper arm has been lifted and not rotated. These rotations are made easily if the shoulder-blades are pressed downwards over the rib-cage and outwards from the spine – the shoulders must never move while the arms rotate in their sockets. Thus the upper back will appear flat and erect and will be able to curve

easily forwards or backwards, allowing the spinal curves to retain their function as shock-absorbers. (See photos 10a and b.)

Slight rotations of the arm in its socket must also be used when the arm travels downwards and backwards or forwards in the *arabesque* line. The arm must never be circled behind at the level of 2nd or 1st position. If it is, the shoulder line will be twisted or displaced in some way.

A somewhat similar adjustment can be made by rotating the lower arm at the elbow or wrist to achieve the ideal 2nd, 1st or 5th positions described above. Admittedly, it is sometimes difficult to obtain this with growing children. But through the practice of well-thought out *ports de bras* and with patience it can be done.

9

11   Natural head movements

on arrival at the desired finish. For example: in a *grand jeté en avant*, the moment the dancer takes off in the air, the head (like the spine) should already have been stretched and curved slightly backwards so that the dancer will land *en fondu*; in an *arabesque allongée*, the dancer is helped to land centrally over the supporting leg and hold that pose. This is not, however, the case with a 'split' or 'flick' *jeté*, where a different action is required.

Similarly when dancing *sauts de basque* to the right and stepping on the right foot before throwing the left upwards to 90° in *écarté* and turning in the air to land on the left foot, the dancer's head and body must very slightly incline to the left. This gives extra pressure and impetus to the left leg as it swings upwards and into a single or double *tour en l'air*. Then as the right leg moves into *retiré*, the left can descend with the weight of the body firmly set over that foot.

Another subtle use of the head to sustain balance happens if a dancer anticipates the direction taken by the working foot so that as it is placed on the floor, the head stretches fully upwards. This should happen in any type of *temps lié*, when the dancer has to step forwards and close in 5th position, *derrière sur les pointes*. The moment that leading foot reaches the floor both body and head must be stretched upwards and erect above that leg and held as the other foot closes behind. A similar anticipation of placing and direction by the head must be used in all types of *pirouette* when danced diagonally or round the stage. (See page 96.)

8   Transfer of Weight: 'Keep those hips still!' (see photos 12a, b, c and d)
The eighth point on which teachers should concentrate is how their students Transfer Weight from one foot to the other, and the exact height of the raised legs in such items as *battements glissés, fondus*, etc. when these are being used as preparations for some transfer. One must insist on the accuracy of such movements for then students will more easily grasp the different ways in which they have to transfer weight through the central line of the body.

There are two types of transfer: firstly from one foot to the other along the floor; and secondly in the air during one of the five jumps which land in one of the five positions or a pose. In either case the weight must be absolutely centred at the moment of transfer. It is for this reason that exact guidance must be given not only for the strength and impetus needed to propel and control the body in some direction, but also for the placing before and after the movement.

To make students understand this important principle teachers must decide as they set their exercises which particular transfer they will use. In other words, they must decide how to place each part of the body to cover space so that it will take the appropriate direction, be given enough impetus and be related to the whole body in order to achieve the desired result.

7   The Head: 'Lift those eyes!' (see photo 11)
A seventh focal point is the head, which can badly disrupt Stance and Balance. A chin drawn inwards may only tilt the head slightly forwards, particularly with growing children who frequently fail to adjust their eye line to their new height. But it can cause neck and shoulder tension, particularly if the arms are thrust backwards. It also affects the whole of the spine, which is unable to stretch fully. If the chin is pressed far inwards it can inhibit all movements of the head which must be free at all times. If the head is not free the focusing of the eyes may affect the inner balance of the ear, which will lead to the loss of speed, accuracy, strength and lightness.

Although it has been said the head leads the body, this must not be interpreted to mean that the head must be in front of the body in every movement. This is far from true. Because it is the heaviest part of the body, it must always seek its true centre whenever the dancer needs to finish a step or pose perfectly balanced over one or two feet. Thus in certain steps the head must anticipate how it will be held

12   Size and direction of step – the fourth girl suggests spacing for a transfer of weight: *a* moving *de face à la seconde*; *b* moving *croisé en avant* or *arrière*; *c* moving *effacé en avant* or *arrière*; *d* different heights to indicate where the foot would fall on a transfer of weight

13   *Epaulements: a croisé devant* and *derrière; b écarté devant* and *derrière; c effacé devant* and *derrière*

9 Height and Extension: 'Follow that toe down!'

The ninth point for teachers to watch arises from the need to Transfer Weight carefully. They must always emphasize the exact direction, height and extension required to cover space. Every exercise at the *barre* is an introduction to the space available for movement within the dancer's own physical capacity. Full use must be made of both the small and large 2nd and 4th positions. Teachers should note carefully the length covered by the outstretched leg and its height from the floor because these determine the size of step to be taken. Teachers should specify the exact amount of stretch or height needed for each particular movement, thus enabling students to discover how to use their capacity to its fullest whilst at the same time adhering to the Principles and Rules common to all dancers. It is particularly important in the various forms of *battements tendus* when the transfer of weight will be along the floor.

A. The smallest space is a mere parting of the feet from 5th to 4th position for an *échappé relevé* or *sauté*.

B. The next, or normal, pace is from 5th position to *pointe tendue devant, à la seconde* or *derrière*, the weight held directly over the supporting leg. When the working heel is carefully lowered, weight should be exactly between the two feet. If the dropping of the working heel *derrière* results in a too large 4th position, the student has possibly not kept the weight firmly over the supporting leg during the stretching outwards; has not kept the 'tail' stretched down to the floor; has pulled the working leg back into the hip socket thus sinking on the supporting side; or has thrown the weight too far backwards instead of merely stretching upwards and slightly adjusting the weight as the working heel descends, so that the weight rests equally over both feet.

The same sized pace should result when the student moves from 5th *demi-plié* into *chassé*, transfers weight and stretches upwards on the new supporting leg. As the working leg stretches, its toe should remain on the same spot as it was when it was supporting.

C. The largest pace is found when the student sinks *en fondu*, simultaneously allowing the working leg to stretch outwards into *pointe tendue devant, à la seconde*, or *derrière*. The student then drops the working heel, whilst keeping the hips at the level indicated by the supporting knee, and then carefully (and gradually) transfers weight through this large *demi-plié* before stretching upwards on the new supporting leg. As soon as the new working leg is fully stretched it, too, will automatically be brought back to the correct *pointe tendue* by the dancer's own strong upward pull of the torso. It should need no further adjustment. (See photos 13a, b and c.)

The various forms of *battements glissés* or *grands battements* prepare students for Transfers of Weight taking place in the air.

D. *Battements glissés en croix*. The working leg should not be raised higher than 20° from the floor, weight firmly fixed over the supporting leg which can be either straight or bent. The working toe then stretches downwards followed by its heel and as the new supporting leg stretches, the other straightens and closes in 5th postion with or without a *demi-plié*. When taken from a *fondu* or *demi-plié* this gives the spacing for a *glissade* which is slightly *sauté*.

E. If, however, the student rises on the supporting leg before transferring weight but without lifting the working leg any higher (i.e. it is at 20° but because of the rise is further from the floor) the space covered will be larger and more suitable for *jetés portés* or *assemblés*.

F. Similarly if students now raise the working leg to 45° or 90° instead of 20° (as in E above) before following the raised toe downwards to transfer weight, the space covered is more suitable for *grands jetés*.

It should also be noted that all the exercises given later for transfer and suggested above help other types of movement. The most helpful rule to use is: always follow the line of the toe downwards if the spacing is to be appropriate to the step or pose that follow and to the individual's own capacity for movement.

The teacher should take careful note of the two ways of opening into *pointe tendue*. The dancer can sink to *demi-plié* before opening to *pointe tendue*, but the leg does not usually extend as far as if he or she simultaneously sinks *en fondu* to *pointe tendue*. The first way is appropriate for all small *glissades à terre*, the second for *glissades sautés* where a stronger impetus must be given to transfer weight. The same idea applies when the dancer slowly and simultaneously sinks *en fondu* raising the working leg to 90°, when it will clearly be seen to be higher than if performed as a *développé* and stretched. Thus if the dancer rises from *en fondu* to a pose and then a *tombé*, a much greater space will be covered.

Similarly when the working leg has to be whipped back into *retiré* at the height of a jump, as in *petits jetés*, then the height of the raised upper leg should not change. Only the shape, because the lower leg is bent back at the knee. Another important factor to note when using *retirés* is the way the leg is raised from 5th position. The tips of the toes should all but rest on the centre front, back or side of the supporting leg, depending on the direction to be followed as the leg unfolds into *développé*. When the upper leg can rise no higher, the lower leg must be opened and raised slightly higher before it is extended to 90° or above for a spacious pose, or before a *tombé*. The muscles responsible for lifting the leg activate the upper part only, so when extension is required others must be freed to take over. It is important to remember this when practising *battements frappés* and *petits battements*, when the upper leg should be held as still as possible and at the correct height for the instep momentarily to rest *sur le cou de pied*. This is particularly so if the following movement is to be *à terre*. However, if *battements fondus* are to be practised and are to be *en l'air*, then the tips of the toes should reach the bottom of the calf and unfold at 45° or at mid-calf if unfolding at 90° or above. Such accuracy of movement helps students to sustain a smooth and equal bend and stretch of both legs. (See photos 14a and b.)

It is also very important to control the height of the raised leg when a dancer has rise into *relevé* with the supporting leg and fall from some held pose (e.g. *devant* at 90°) into another pose (perhaps *arabesque*). If the raised leg is brought in any way backwards towards the supporting one during the transfer the whole balance of the body will be strained and, as before, the spinal curves will be too tense to act as shock-absorbers, their proper function.

Timing Movement Musically: 'Listen to the music!'

Music should never be a mere time-keeper. Students should learn to respond sensitively to the timing of each detail both technically and musically. If not, their movements do not make sense.

In many shops and homes today music is just a background to which children rarely listen with attention. Nor do they listen properly if they dance continually

14 Position of the foot *sur le cou de pied*

to the same set pieces that are recommended with a syllabus. They may even contradict the beat if they wish to show off more turns or a higher jump for which neither teacher nor musician has allowed time.

Children in Elementary class certainly require steady tempo, clear beat and regular phrasing. But even within these limits there can be fine variations. For example: a *pas de basque* in 3/4 can be rephrased 2/4 – and the difference in quality will be evident immediately. At Intermediate level, the phrasing should become more subtle. At an Advanced stage uneven time-signatures, e.g. 5/4 or 7/8, or irregular phrases, should be introduced to challenge the ability of those who wish to become professional dancers. For on the stage they may have to interpret highly complex rhythms, phrases and tonalities. The music of Stravinsky, once considered difficult, does not in fact present these problems. Even young children can experience the excitement of his *Rite of Spring*, because its insistent rhythmic beat is something they respond to once they have really listened.

A gradually quickening tempo, even at early stages of training, is invaluable in teaching how to gain speed. Ninette de Valois in one of her lectures made the point: 'It is important to remember that as a dancer gains speed the quality and accuracy of the step must not change, but the space it fills will become less. Therefore accuracy of position, placing the direction of every detail in each step is everything.' This is why it is so often important to practise all types of *petits sauts*, *batterie* and *pointe* work with no, or scarcely any, *demi-pliés*. The dancer must rely on the flexibility and strength of every part of the foot and ankle-joint.

Unlike Fokine, not many teachers today give much thought to the way in which directions as to timing are given to students and to that most important colleague, the musician. The words used, their emphasis and the tone of voice should convey time-signatures, speed, quality and even particular details within the phrasing required. Thought has to be given to which word or words need emphasis to point out the importance of a step or pose. Even a count of 'one, two and a three, four' should convey the timing of an *enchaînement*. Once the order of steps has been spoken and demonstrated simultaneously, it should be possible for teachers not to shout orders or corrections through the music.

Indeed, no-one should give order to dancers like a sergeant-major. It is not surprising that prospective teachers are sometimes encouraged to have lessons in voice production, particularly if they have had a professional career where the nervous tension of always being on show – so to speak – frequently results in a tightening of the vocal chords.

Timing Movement Physically: 'Bend and stretch those legs together!'

It will be noted that I have several times mentioned that movements must be performed simultaneously, e.g. the *fondu* on the supporting leg and *retiré* of the working one followed during *battements fondus* by the simultaneous stretching of the supporting leg upwards and the working leg outwards particularly before a Transfer of Weight. The two actions must be meticulously timed to reach the greatest stretch at the same moment. Several other steps require even more sensitive timing for simultaneous action. The examples that follow are perhaps the most important and take much practice to perfect as so much depends upon the perfect adjustment of weight and upon the involvement of the whole body. In other words, there must be an absolute Co-ordination of all parts which if suitably accompanied by the musician, is very rewarding to watch, Cf. Ashton's *Symphonic Variations*.

A *Ronds de jambe à terre en tournant*, where the circling and supporting legs should arrive simultaneously, in *pointe tendue à la seconde* each time the dancer faces a new corner of the studio (in other words, a new front). The *rond* begins *pointe tendue devant* and circles *en dehors* as the dancer makes a quarter turn to arrive with *pointe tendue à la seconde* because the supporting leg has pivoted to reach the new front. The working leg then circles behind, before moving through 1st position to repeat another *rond*. The actual quarter turn on the supporting leg is made as the working leg passes through 1st position.

B *Adage*. The swift change from one pose to another during an *adage* presents difficulties in adjusting both alignment and/or *épaulement* if legs and arms do not work simultaneously. For example: a dancer who moves from *écarté effacé devant* at 90°, through *retiré* to *arabesque allongée* while still keeping *effacé* can only manage the sequence satisfactorily if both legs bend and stretch simultaneously as the supporting leg pivots. At the same time, a similar co-ordination takes place in the arms which move from 4th to 1st position and then to 1st or 2nd *arabesque* lines.

C All *pirouettes*, no matter of what kind and after the appropriate preparation, need the simultaneous action of both legs as well as of the rest of the body. The legs must rise and arrive at the correct position at the very moment when the turn begins, e.g. following *demi-plié* into *relevé*, the working leg must be raised directly into *retiré*. The impetus for the turn must begin just before the dancer makes a quarter turn. As the turn begins, he or she must pull up every muscle of the legs and torso, particularly on the supporting side.

To prove the effectiveness of the above views on spacing, transfer of weight and timing, teachers should also study how to phrase steps and poses accurately and musically into *enchaînements*, how to present themselves and their techniques to a class, how to teach growing boys and girls – above all, how to create a class from all that they have learnt as students and performers.

Standing in Front of the Class

Teachers should demonstrate as accurately as possible and, if they possess any particular idiosyncrasy, it must be eliminated before facing a class. This is essential when teaching children, who pick up the slightest habit. However, the main task is to make pupils use their brains and bodies for themselves.

Teachers should always face their class and never demonstrate with their backs. I have even found it valuable if I wish my students to commence with the right foot front, to begin with my right and not my left foot, which is customary. Admittedly I only do this with Advanced classes. But I do sometimes make children dance in a circle, all commencing with the same foot, which helps to give them a sense of independence and is valuable if the *enchaînement* also makes patterns such as in and out of a circle as well as round and in reverse.

Facing the class also means that the teacher's eyes can always pick on, firstly, faults arising from a misunderstanding of the exercise by the whole class and, secondly (perhaps), the one student whose movement does not conform to the pattern laid down.

1 Facing the Mirror

The practice of students facing a mirror and assessing their own faults can be very valuable if adopted in moderation. But it can lead to the development of 'mirror dancers', that is, those who do not consider or feel the need to project to an audience the line and, maybe, the quality and expression of a movement. This is because they are only interested in themselves and always turn their heads and bodies to see if they approve of their own efforts.

If possible teachers should continually change the front. This gives pupils a much better idea of how to feel the changing alignments and *épaulements* in relationship to an audience. It also makes for greater accuracy, placing and spacing. The dancer's fascination with self is nowhere better demonstrated than in Robbins' *Afternoon of a Faun* where the two dancers' sudden awareness of each other as boy and girl is beautifully revealing of the change in quality when people become interested in others. (See photos 15a and b.)

a

15 'Mirror dancers' – Robbins' *Afternoon of the Faun* (Bryony Brind and Ashley Page): *a* Self interested; *b* Recognition

b

2 Differences between Boys and Girls (see photos 16a and b)

Ideally boys and girls should be taught separately in their early training. But as this is rarely possible, it is important for the teacher to make clear the differences, particularly in the use of the arms. Boys' arms, like girls', must work freely in their sockets and without tension, so that it becomes easier to control the upper back as the boys grow. But it is essential to see that the boys' arms are held as widely open as possible – though still rounded – so that the shoulders look broader as the chest is expanded sideways and outwards through correct breathing.   Boys do not have the same flexibility in the pelvic area as girls. Because of this and because of the way boys grow – they do not change shape as girls do, they only grow taller and broader – it is essential that correct Stance is established at the beginning of training. Much greater attention must therefore be paid to the pelvic area in growing boys. At this stage it is far better to keep the muscles under tight control so that the hips do not twist and the torso does not sink into the legs, even if this means losing something of the Turn-out and the height of the working leg. By such control the muscles of the inner and outer thigh, of the pelvis and stomach can be strengthened and stretched, and the over-development of the quadriceps and buttock muscles prevented.

In my experience most boys' legs – particularly the lower half – seem to grow before their bodies and if this happens quickly control in this area is lost. If the same thing happens to the feet – and I have had cases – boys have great difficulty in finding their new centre over the supporting foot until the legs, too, have grown. This type of growth usually means that boys' feet need much harder work than girls.

It is important that growing girls learn control over hips and upper torso and over the height of the working leg. But it is perhaps even more important to ensure that the rib-cage is nowhere strained upwards and backwards by the shoulder-blades being drawn together. Or by the shoulders being brought forwards so that the chest is narrowed. Both result in very shallow breathing as they do not allow the ribs to expand, nor the arms to move freely. The rib-cage should be lifted easily upwards from underneath by slimming the waist. Thus the spine is not tensed in any way. Also – and at a fast growing stage – both head and arms can stretch outwards from the body.

3 Tempo and Pattern for Growing Children

It is of utmost importance that teachers of growing children take particular care over the timing and placing of each step in an *enchaînement*. The tempo must be such that it gives them time to fit all in comfortably without having to rush their movements and thus cut corners. The steps should be clearly defined by distinct

a

b

16 Positions of the feet – also in *demi-* and full *plié: a* in first or second positions; *b* in fourth or fifth positions

closing and/or transferring of weight through one of the five positions. No *enchaînement* should find them standing too long on one leg. It is far better to insist on slow *demi-grands ronds de jambe* than on one full *rond* at a faster pace, particularly if their growth is fast. If complicated *batterie* is given, then it is better to break it up a little by using *changements*, *soubresauts*, *glissades*, etc. as preparations. And always remember, as has already been stated, that it is better to lose the height of the working leg than the stability of the supporting one. This leg is like an anchor and properly used should ensure, with subtle movements of the upper torso, that the weight is centrally balanced at all times.

4 Arms and Hands

All too often teachers concentrate on the legs. But in front of a class of children they themselves should take great care of the way they hold and place their own arms. In fact keeping their own arms lower than usual in 1st and 2nd positions is essential, particularly for young children who are shorter than they are. Children look upwards at their teachers and watch the facial expression, which demands their obedience. They raise their arms to what they believe is the same height. As a result the arms are usually too high.

The teachers' arms should also be more consciously rounded so that the straightening of the arms in an *arabesque* line is more clearly visible.

If Stance and the use of the arms are to be correct, teachers must insist that the placing of the hand on the *barre* is correct and appropriate to the individual. If the rounded arms are held outwards in a position midway between 1st and 2nd positions (i.e. 45° to the body), the elbows should be drawn inwards until they all but touch the sides. One hand should now be directed forwards at that same angle and placed ON TOP OF THE *BARRE* – not grasping the *barre*.

Few *barres* are at the appropriate height for all children in class. Nevertheless the hand on the *barre* must be seen in front and NOT at the side of the body. It must also have freedom to move slightly forwards when any movement above 20° is performed to the back. This adjustment is essential when moving into any *arabesque*. Today the leg is expected to rise higher than 90°, therefore the arm must move slightly forwards, otherwise correct alignment is lost. The old idea that the hand on the *barre* never moved no matter what the dancer performed was what restricted the height of the leg and the flexibility of the body. Today's choreographers require a full range of movement, therefore dancers must prepare in class. Also, and more important, if they attempt to keep the hand in the same place in *grand battement derrière*, the resulting tension in shoulders and spine can lead to groin and back troubles because the pelvis has been rocked or twisted and NOT gently tilted. (See photos 17a and b.)

a

17   *Arabesques: a à terre* and *en l'air; b en l'air*

b

18

5 Eyes

Another vital adjustment has to be made as children grow. This is the height at which they focus their eyes. Unless they are firmly guided to raise their heads and re-focus at a higher level, particularly at times of fast growth, they continue to focus on the same spot as during a more stable period, usually when they first began training. If this stretch upwards is not continually stressed, the head loses its freedom as well as the shoulders and arms, which tend to contract inwards and forwards. And if, at this point, teachers demand 'shoulders back', the result will be a 'poking chin' and not a stretching of the head away from the neck (i.e. the cervical spine).

One way to help growing children to re-focus their eyes to a proper level is never to allow them to stand in the same place at the *barre* or in the centre. The plight of a fast-growing boy who always works behind one growing slowly has to be seen to be believed. I fully realise that this continual moving about can be difficult and is usually disliked by the boys themselves. Girls do not seem to mind so much. But a constant change of place does help to improve Stance and Placing and very often gives greater certainty to the movements.

6 Dance Uniform

SHOES

Teachers should take a proper interest in their pupils' dress, particularly the shoes as these are vital to their well-being and part of the discipline. As children grow fast it is always difficult to ensure a proper fit at all times. But never allow children to work in shoes too tight across the metatarsal arches or too short for the toes. When the foot is fully pointed, the end of the leather sole of 'flatties' should come to the end of the wearer's heel. This is most important later when girls have to fit *pointe* shoes. When the foot is flat and taking weight a slight pressure of the teacher's hand will indicate if the metatarsal arch or toes are being cramped in any way. If they are, it may mean that the shoe is altogether too short (because the draw-string has been pulled up too tightly) and the pads of the toes cannot lie flat on the floor.

Boys always seem to prefer very tight shoes when growing, possibly because their ankles and arches often weaken. They are prone to pull up their draw-string much too tightly. This often results in the big toes being curled upwards and thus the weight placed too far back on the heels. Similarly on no account should girls' shoe ribbons be tied too tightly. If they are sewn on properly at an angle tilting forwards then wrapped round the ankle like a slim bandage, the back of a well-fitting shoe should not slip off the heel.

DRESS

Leotards and footless tights over cotton socks are ideal garments for both boys and girls. (Alternatives for boys are footless tights, cotton socks and vests.) Both should also wear a narrow belt or piece of broad elastic at waist level as this helps to indicate whether or not the stomach and other muscles are being stretched upwards and away from the hips. As boys mature they fancy the modern fashion of placing the belt round the hips and roll their tights down over this. It is then useless, particularly as when they grow fast they are usually very unstable in this area; the belt soon gets moved and can interfere with the leg movements.

HAIR

Girls' hair should be kept tidy and away from the nape of the neck. It is not good to wear a head-band tied down over the ears. This can and usually does inhibit head movements in the same way as a bun tied tightly at the nape of the neck. Boys' hair should never be allowed to be so long that it gets in their eyes when they turn, or impairs their vision if they refuse to lift the head as they should.

7 The Class Prepared

Teachers should always face their class with a lesson already prepared and with a clear idea of which steps and poses are to be taught and practised. In other words, they should have two aims in view. Firstly, each step should be analysed and practised in some detail in its basic form. The line and direction it takes should be demonstrated. Any difficulty it presents should be explained, particularly the way in which all parts of the body must co-ordinate to achieve the desired result. Secondly, each step or pose should be practised in as many *enchaînements* as possible that are suitable for the age and standard of the pupils. In other words, teachers must design a properly balanced class.

A properly balanced class should exercise the entire body by utilising the four movements of dance of which John Weaver (1723) said its anatomical structure was capable: to bend, stretch, rise and turn. It should also cover the seven movements of dance designated by Noverre (1760): to bend, stretch, rise, jump, glide, dart and turn. Petipa in his Vocabulary (1890) divided the steps and poses into seven categories and gave the purpose of each: preparatory or auxiliary steps, elevation, *batterie*, *pirouettes*, poses, *ports de bras* and *pointes*. There is plenty of material on which to base a varied and balanced class.

Through the years each school has devised its own order and pattern of exercises so that what is practised at the *barre* guides the student towards what is danced in the centre. There are several variations in the order, but it matters little where an exercise comes as long as it finds a place. Nevertheless it is not wise to concentrate on too much of any one step nor to give energetic, fast or large stretching exercises and movements until bodies have been thoroughly warmed up by slower and more careful *terre à terre* work.

The content of the classes in Part Two has been slightly curtailed for reasons of space. They are intended to cover as many points as possible and to last between one and one-and-a-quarter hours, no longer. Also in order to help teachers understand how one exercise is developed from Elementary to Intermediate and Advanced standard, I adhere to the same sequence for all three and number them similarly. By so doing I hope to show how changing time-signatures, changing tempos and changes in alignment and/or *épaulement* alter the qualities of even the simplest movement.

Although each of the classes concentrates on one Principle throughout each section, I also try to show the development of one step or another from its basic form in the Elementary class to increasing difficulties in the Intermediate and Advanced stages. Thus a class concentrating on Stance can also be a lesson in how to dance *glissades* and *assemblés*, or a class on Turn-out can stress *pas de basque* or *pas de bourrée*. All such steps are prepared during *barre*-work.

This is how Asaf Messerer, following Vaganova's example, worked out his classes for the Bolshoi ballet. Starting on Mondays he introduced the chosen steps in their simplest form, believing that after a day's rest or only a quick warm-up before the Sunday matinée (the usual Soviet practice) his dancers needed to get back to basics and the mood to work. By Friday his *enchaînements* retained their same pattern and content, but were scarcely recognisable. *Batterie*, *pirouettes*, *grande élévation*, etc. had been added. And, as in every class I ever attended given by important Russian teachers, danced in reverse. How well I remember the order, 'Now reverse!', just as we were finishing some complicated beaten step moving forwards – and 'reverse' we did! This was when Astafieva or Vaganova would often point out that we had covered great space when moving forwards, but had not travelled so far backwards. Why? Our legs should have reached the same distance, no matter which way we went, had we been working properly.

8   Development of Memory and Stamina

It was in Vaganova's classes that I encountered the infinite variety of *temps liés*. She had sixteen versions which could be glided, stepped, darted or jumped. She would also sometimes add other steps, usually at the end of a phrase: for example, *battements tendus devant* and *derrière* after we had moved forwards, and *à la 2nde* after we had moved sideways; or a *port de bras* after starting with a *pirouette en dehors* and another after a *pirouette en dedans*.

It is by varying the length and content of *enchaînements* that students gradually develop their ability to memorise them, as well as their stamina for longer musical and dance phrases. At the Elementary stage no *enchaînement* should be too long, though it should be capable of being danced to the right and then to the left without a pause – and then be danced in reverse. As students progress, it is important to increase the length and difficulty of the *enchaînements*: for example, the teacher should extend a *changement* or an *assemblé* into a *changement* or *assemblé battu*. The class will then begin to understand how a simple step can be developed into more complicated forms and yet still follow the basic principles and rules.

The practice of repeating *enchaînements* to right and left ensures that all movements are distributed equally throughout the dancer's body and over the stage. Classical dance demands that the audience must always be able to recognise the lines drawn individually and collectively on the stage, viewed from any angle. Students must be made aware and constantly reminded that every member of a *corps de ballet* has a part to play. Every step, pose and phrase of a dance has its own pattern and direction – the dancer should be able to move into any place in the line or pattern and to start with either foot. I have occasionally found it very rewarding to divide a class into groups or lines of three or four dancers. The groups then dance *enchaînements*, variously starting with the right or left foot, perhaps passing through each other's lines, circling in opposite directions or standing at different angles. Within a group, dancers can face each other or move back to back, dissolve into a new design or change partners. All this helps students to understand the value of placing themselves in correct alignment or *épaulement* one to another. It also makes them understand, almost better than any other method, the importance of timing their movements both physically and musically so that the personal contribution becomes part of the whole.

Final Words of Advice

Yet despite the suggestions made in the last paragraph, the teacher must avoid any attempt to be a choreographer. The latter creates dance from living material and expects the dancers to be sympathetic and adaptable to the purpose and design. The teacher's role is to ensure that the students are fully conversant with the Rules laid down for classical dance and that they maintain the basic principles of Stance, Turn-out, Placing, Laws of balance, Transfer of weight and Co-ordination. Any deviation from normal practice made by the choreographer will then be instantly recognised so that necessary changes can be made. As Ninette de Valois has said, 'It is better to have a rule to break than no rule at all if chaos is not to reign in class-room and stage.'. The teacher must be the one to 'call the tune' in the class-room, to spot any deviation, to observe the student's response and to see that the students' movements are timed technically and physically with the music in order to fill the studio with dance.

Let the class begin!

18 Let it begin! – opening of the Bluebirds' *pas de deux* from *The Sleeping Beauty* (Ravenna Tucker and Phillip Broomhead)

PART TWO
The Classes

19 *Pas courus en avant* from *La Bayadère* (Julie Rose)

20 *Pas courus en arrière*, the Songbird in *The Sleeping Beauty* (Julie Rose)

Notes on the Classes

It is usual to commence all exercises at the *barre* with the right foot and this is the convention for all the following classes. But I have found it invaluable to insist that students sometimes start with the left foot as this benefits the left-handed and those with legs of uneven length. It is also useful to commence sometimes in 3rd or 5th position as this helps to establish Stance and the centring of weight. Standing always in 1st can prevent beginners from understanding the need always to balance over the supporting leg.

If no specific *port de bras* is given, any simple conventional one should be used to maintain co-ordination of all parts of the body. However, for the ninth exercise of centre practice in each Elementary class, I have given *ports de bras*. It does not *have* to be the final exercise, but its place in my class is a tribute to my many Russian teachers who always ended thus. This was followed by the *révérence* to both teacher and pianist.

It may be thought that I have to some extent neglected *pointe*-work as I give no specific classes. But from time to time I note where certain exercises should also be practised *sur les pointes* after they have been introduced on *demi-pointes*. In the ninth exercise of *barre*-work, I sometimes suggest a preparatory exercise for *pointes*.

The time signatures which I have indicated for Elementary and Intermediate classes are only suggestions except in those few cases where exact timing and emphasis outwards or inwards on the beat are essential for the necessary impetus behind a movement. In the Advanced classes, however, I give more exact notes on the time signature and timing in order to emphasise the particular qualities of a movement so danced.

N.B. The photographs in each section illustrate the Principle which underlies the set of exercises and not any particular step, as the dancers were asked to demonstrate a choreographer's version of the movement rather than the purely classical model.

The basic order of the classes
(there will be a few deviations)

AT THE *BARRE*

1 *Pliés* – in various forms, with and without *ports de bras*.
2 *Battements tendus* – in various forms, with particular emphasis on the need to space a step and on the transfer of weight.
3 *Battements glissés* – usually a faster and lighter form of *tendus* and also for landing from jumps.
4 *Ronds de jambe à terre* – in various forms, with particular emphasis on spacing and on the transfer of weight.
5 *Grands battements* – in various forms, including *tombés* and stretching or holding movements.
6 *Battements frappés* or exercises to introduce jumps or beats.
7 *Petits battements* or exercises that prepare for beats or *pirouettes*.
8 *Adage* – to introduce all sustained and stretching movements.
9 Practice for *pointe*-work or stretching.

IN THE CENTRE

1 *Petit adage* – usually repeating in the centre movements from **1** to **3** of *barre*-work.
2 *Petit adage* – usually repeating in the centre movements from **1** to **5** of *barre*-work.
3 *Grand adage* – using elements from *adage* at the *barre* (**8** above) and occasionally from **5**, **6** and **7**.
4 *Pirouettes* – *en dehors* and *en dedans*, with and without *fouettés*, finishing with and without poses.
5 *Petit allegro* – simple warm-up jumps, usually from two feet to two feet, two feet to one foot, or one foot to two feet.
6 *Petit allegro* – introducing *batterie*.
7 *Grand allegro* – the simpler forms of *grande élévation*.
8 *Grand allegro* – more complicated steps of *grande élévation*, with *batterie* and/or turns.
9 *Ports de bras* (for Elementary centre practice), *pirouettes en diagonale* or *en manège* in various forms. Also *tours en l'air* (for boys).

Stance

PRINCIPLE

'The dancer gets the best results when the spine has been straightened to its fullest. It must not be stiffened as its curves must continue to act as shock-absorbers.'

Throughout this first set of classes Stance is the main concern. Care should be taken to ensure that the weight is held up away from the waist at the beginning and end of every exercise, so that the 'gap' (or 'muscular corset') is maintained throughout, thus strengthening all the muscles in the pelvis, stomach and upper torso and ensuring that the weight is fully centred over one or both feet.

RULES TO FOLLOW

A The head must always lead the movement and the eyes focus on the line to be made. (See also pages 10 and 96.)

B The feet always find the head, the head never finds the feet.

C Ensure that the pelvis does not twist and is kept as still as possible. It is essential that the legs and arms never over- or under-cross the central line of the body.

D The arms must always move freely in their sockets and be stretched sideways (though rounded) away from the body so that the shoulder-blades can flatten on the rib-cage. This ensures correct breathing. In addition, if the arms are raised from 1st or 2nd to 5th or 4th, the elbows must not be allowed to fall inwards, but must be held in a correct relationship to the shoulders. These must be kept down and well stretched outwards. This is particularly important in any practice of the 5th *port de bras* (see page 40).

FOCAL POINTS

1 The pelvic area (see page 5).
2 Feet and legs (see pages 5, 6 and 7).
3 Upper torso (see page 6).

N.B. Although this first class was particularly aimed at boys, who must establish correct Stance in the first stages of training, it also proved to be valuable for girls who have to adjust as they grow in order always to stand correctly whatever the changes in their physique.

(see photos 19, 20, 21, 22, 23a and b)

Preparatory To find correct Stance [4 bars of 3/4 or 2 bars of 4/4.]

1. Stand erect, feet parallel and slightly apart, toes facing forwards. Place one hand on *barre* (see page 18), with the other *bras bas*.

2. Rise on *demi-pointes*, weight carried upwards and forwards, legs and spine fully stretched. Raise arm to 1st. (i.e. straighten cervical and thoracic spine.)

3. Drop heels without displacing line of body in relation to toes, thus pulling 'tail' downwards which tilts the pelvis very slightly upwards. (i.e. flatten lumbar spine.)

4. Turn feet outwards as far as possible from hip joints keeping heels together and pulling torso strongly upwards, whilst opening arm to 2nd. This flattens the shoulder-blades. Adjust the head to the new centre.

    From this position and with fully stretched legs, raise and lower heels twice without bending the knees, i.e. to *demi-pointes*.

This Stance exercise should be practised as a preparation for several others at the *barre* until it becomes habitual.

1 Stance to be held during *pliés* [8 bars of 3/4 or 4 bars of 4/4.]

1. Repeat the exercise above to find correct Stance.

2. 2 *demi-pliés* and 1 full *plié* in 1st. Turn legs in. It is essential to see that the knees relax before they bend, i.e. instead of being tightly drawn upwards, the muscles must allow the knee-cap to drop slightly before the descent.

3. Repeat 1, rising once only, and stretch to *pointe tendue à la 2nde*.

4. Repeat 2 *demi-* and one full *plié* in 2nd.

5 – 8. Repeat 3 and 4, but after *pointe tendue* close in 3rd or 5th.

Stance – Intermediate *Barre*

Stance – Advanced *Barre*

1 *Pliés* [Slow waltz in 16 bar phrases or 6/8 in 4 bar phrases.]

Commence in 5th.

1. *Battement tendu* closing 1st, *demi-plié*; 2 full *pliés* and *ports de bras*, bending straight forwards to 90° (see page 40).
2. Repeat as 1, but moving to 2nd and bending sideways to the *barre*.
3. Repeat 4th opposite 5th, bending backwards with the head slightly turned over the same shoulder as the foot in front, arm in *arabesque*.
4. Repeat in 5th, circling *ports de bras* (see page 40).

1 *Pliés* [Slow waltz, 8 bars; 6/8 or 4/4 in 2 bar phrases.]

Commence in 1st. Note arm movement.

1. 2 *demi-pliés*; whilst knees are bent on second, raise heels; arms 1st.
2. Stretch knees upwards to full *demi-pointes*, tightening all inner and outer thigh and pelvic muscles, arms 5th.
3. Full *plié* sinking heels before bending knees, arm moving from 5th to 1st, 2nd and *bras bas*.

Repeat in 2nd, 4th opposite 5th and 5th.

2a Stance during *battements tendus* (to strengthen the 'muscular corset') [4/4.]

Commence in 1st, 3rd or 5th.

1. Transfer weight to supporting leg, stretching to *pointe tendue devant*, toe in line with heel, stance correct, leg as turned out as possible, *bras bas* and raise to 1st.
2. Drop heel by bending foot at ankle and transfer weight equally over both feet, keeping the spine and both legs fully stretched, arms 2nd.
3. Raise heel, transferring weight backwards to the supporting leg.
4. Close 1st, 3rd or 5th. Drop arm to *bras bas*.

Repeat *en croix*, then repeat dropping into *demi-pliés* in all the open positions.

N.B. It is also valuable to change feet after each close, moving *devant*, *derrière* and *à la 2nde*, twice. This ensures that there is a proper transfer of weight to the supporting leg each time the *pointe tendue* begins.

or

2b *Battements tendus* as preparation for *glissades* [2 bars of 4/4.]

Commence with both hands on *barre*, in 1st position.

1. 2 *tendus à la 2nde*, closing 3rd or 5th *devant* and *derrière demi-plié*.
2. Holding *fondu*, stretch right *pointe tendue à la 2nde*, transfer to right *fondu*, stretching left *pointe tendue*. Transfer to left *fondu*, re-stretching left – repeat the transfer and close 1st, stretching the knees.

N.B. It is important to keep the hips still and parallel to the floor during the transfer and to use the full stretch of each leg in turn. When a smooth transfer has been mastered, this should be practised *en croix*, hips and shoulders always facing the same plane and parallel to each other and to the floor.

3 *Battements glissés en croix* [2/4 or waltz.]

Commence in 1st, 3rd or 5th.

Practise as in **2a** above but use 2 *glissés devant* and on a third drop into open position in *demi-plié* and re-stretch the knees before closing. The working leg must not rise higher than 20° and the *glissés* taken slowly so that the heel can be seen to follow the toe down in one continuous movement and to return along the same line. (See page 13.)

4 *Ronds de jambe à terre, en dehors* and *en dedans* [4 bar phrases.]

Commence in 1st, 3rd or 5th.

1. Holding weight firmly over supporting leg, stretch to *pointe tendue devant*, circle *à la 2nde* and *derrière*, close 1st. Hold each point momentarily and raise arm through 1st to 2nd.
2. Pass through to *pointe tendue devant* and *fondu*, repeating *rond*.
3 – 4. 8 *ronds en dehors*. Ensure that the working leg passes correctly through 1st and never over- or under-crosses. Do not allow the hips to twist.

Repeat the whole exercise moving *en dedans*.

N.B. Encourage the use of simple *ports de bras*. During the quick *ronds* raise arm from *bras bas* to 1st, 5th and open to 2nd. When moving *en dedans*, raise the arms from 2nd to 5th and down to 1st and *bras bas*. If the head leads the movement it will move naturally into the correct angles. There must be continuity of movement and not the striking of a pose.

Stance – Intermediate *Barre*

2 *Battements tendus* [4/4 or steady 2/4 in 2 or 4 bar phrases.]
Commence in 5th.
1. *Battement tendu devant*, drop heel, re-point toe, close 5th *devant*.
2. *Pointe tendue devant*, curl toes, re-point toes and close 5th *derrière*.
3 – 4. Repeat *derrière* and *à la 2nde*, then 1 set *en croix*, closing each in 5th *demi-plié*.

N.B. Note the difference between bending the foot at the ankle and curling the toes and ensure that the foot is correctly re-pointed.

3 *Battements glissés* [2/4 in 2 bar phrases.]
Commence in 1st.
1. 3 *glissés à la 2nde* and a fourth closing 5th *demi-plié*.
2. 4 *glissés devant*, fourth closing 5th *demi-plié*.

Repeat in reverse. Repeat twice in all.

4 *Ronds de jambe à terre* [Waltz or 6/8 in 8 or 4 bar phrases.]
Commence in 5th.
1. Simultaneously *fondu* to *pointe tendue devant* and circle *à la 2nde* stretching the supporting leg; repeat circling from side *en fondu* to *derrière*; *fondu* and pass through 1st stretching into 2 *ronds en dehors*.
2. 4 *ronds en dehors* and 1 slow *en fondu*, finishing *pointe tendue derrière*, arm 5th and stretching slightly forwards so that an almost straight line can be seen from pointed toe through the spine to the head.

Recover and immediately repeat in reverse (*en dedans*).
The final stretch being seen from the front toe to the head, with arms open 5th.

Stance – Advanced *Barre*

2 *Battements tendus* to lengthen and stretch inner and outer thigh muscles [4/4 in 2 bar or waltz in 4 bar phrases.]
Commence in 5th.
1. *Tendu devant* closing 5th, low *développé* to *pointe tendue devant*, close 5th.
2. Repeat *tendu* closing *demi-plié* and with *relevé* on *développé*. Repeat *en croix*. Repeat whole.

N.B. Once the toe has reached the floor after the *développé*, it must not leave it even though the supporting leg is on *demi-pointe*. Keep the hips square.

3 *Battements glissés* [3/4 in 4 bar or Tarantella in 2 bar phrases.]
Commence in 1st, 3rd or 5th.
2 *glissés devant*, second closing 5th *demi-plié*, *relevé* with slow *développé devant*, step *en avant* and close *sur demi-pointes*, lower heels.

Repeat *derrière* and twice *à la 2nde*, moving away and towards *barre*.

4 *Ronds de jambe à terre* [Waltz in 4 bar phrases.]
Commence in 5th.
1. Stretch to *pointe tendue à la 2nde*, drop heel, re-point toe for 2 *ronds en dehors*, finishing *pointe tendue à la 2nde*.
2 – 3 – 4. Repeat twice. Close 5th *devant* and *développé à la 2nde* with a rise. Close 5th *derrière*.

Repeat the whole exercise *en dedans*.

5 _Grands battements en croix_ [4/4, with the accent on the 1st and 3rd beats of each bar.]

Commence in 1st, 3rd or 5th.

1. Throw fully stretched leg _devant_ to 90°.
2. Drop to small 4th opposite 5th, transferring weight equally over both feet.
3. Transfer weight back to supporting leg, raising the other to 45°.
4. Close 1st, 3rd or 5th.

Repeat the exercise _à la 2nde, derrière_ and _à la 2nde_.

N.B. It is essential that the spine and head are fully stretched, with the weight held upwards when moving _devant_ and _à la 2nde_; also that the upper torso and head curve correctly into an _arabesque_ when moving _derrière_.

6 _Battements frappés en croix_. An introduction as preparation for any exercise starting _sur le cou de pied_ [4/4.]

Introduction. (1) _Pointe tendue à la 2nde_. (2) Bend foot up at a right angle to the leg. (3) Place the foot across the supporting ankle so that the instep rests across and above the ankle bone. (4) Point the foot straight downwards so that the tips of the toes touch the floor. (This can be difficult if the feet are small, but should be tried.)

1. Thrust the fully stretched leg _devant_ so that the pads of the toes brush the floor with a strong accent outwards while the leg rises no higher than 20°.
2. Return the foot _sur le cou de pied_.

Repeat _à la 2nde, derrière_ and _à la 2nde_, keeping the working knee at the same height and degree of turn-out. The lower leg and foot do most of the work.

7 _Petits battements sur le cou de pied_ as a preparation for _batterie_ [2/4 in 4 bar phrases.]

Commence using **6** as a preparation.

1 – 2. (1-2, 1-2) Beat foot _derrière – devant_ twice, with the tips of the toes brushing the floor so that movement out and in comes from the knee only. The upper leg must be held as still as possible.
3. Close 3rd or 5th _devant demi-plié_.
4. _Retiré passé_ stretching supporting leg to _sur le cou de pied derrière_.

Repeat in reverse. Then repeat with _retiré passé sauté_.

N.B. It is important to emphasise the stretch of the foot from _sur le cou de pied_ to _retiré_ and ensure that it does not sickle inwards or outwards as it travels upwards. The knee should be slightly pressed backwards or forwards to help maintain turn-out as the position changes. It is also very important to see that the working foot does cross in front of or behind the supporting ankle if _batterie_ is to be clean and correct.

Stance – Intermediate *Barre*

5 *Grands battements* [4/4 in 2 bar phrases – accent up on beat.]

Commence in 5th.

  2 *battements devant* at 90°, closing 5th, 1 *battement devant*, closing *retiré* and then 5th.

Repeat *en croix* and then repeat *sur les pointes*.

N.B. Ensure that the weight is firmly placed on both feet between the *battements sur les pointes*. Never allow the working leg to shorten by NOT pressing the toes into the floor.

6 *Battements frappés doublés en croix*

  As for Elementary Barre **6** but beat *devant – derrière*, or as suitable between *frappés*. The accent must be well outwards and the beat clean across the ankle.

Repeat twice on flat foot and twice *sur les demi-pointes*.

7 *Petits battements* as practice for *batterie* [Slow 2/4 in 2 bar phrases.]

Commence *sur le cou de pied*. (Use Introduction to Elementary Barre **6**, page 30.)

  (and 1 – and 2 – and 3) beat *derrière – devant* three times accenting *devant*.

  (and 4) beat *devant – derrière*.

Repeat in reverse.

This exercise introduces the beats for 4 *entrechats quatre* and 1 *changement battu*.

Repeat 4 times in all, ensuring the work comes mostly from the knee downwards.

Stance – Advanced *Barre*

5 *Grands battements* [Polonaise in 2 bar phrases; note timing.]

Commence in 5th.

  1. (1) Throw *devant* to 90°. (2) Hold. (3) Close 5th. Repeat.
  2. (1) Throw *devant*. (2) Hold. (3) *Retiré*.
      (1) *Développé devant*. (2) Hold. (3) Close.

Repeat *derrière* and *à la 2nde* followed by 4 *retirés passés*, holding the *retiré* on the second beat of each bar.

6 and 7 *Frappés* as preparation for *cabrioles* [Steady 2/4 in 2 bar phrases.]

Commence *sur le cou de pied*.

  1. 2 *frappés devant*, the second closing 5th *demi-plié, glissé devant* with a spring off the supporting leg and beating it against the raised leg whilst in the air. Close 5th *demi-plié*.
  2. Snatch foot *sur le cou de pied* into 2 *frappés à la 2nde*, close 5th *devant demi-plié* and *petit assemblé* to 5th *derrière*. Repeat *frappés* and *cabriole derrière* and *frappés* with *assemblé*.

Repeat the whole exercise.

N.B. Ensure that the weight is correctly centred so that the head and upper torso can anticipate the direction that the *cabriole* will take. When moving *à la 2nde*, both body and head must be erect and the jump upwards, both feet coming together in the air before landing *demi-plié*. It is not advisable to practise *cabriole à la 2nde* as this is a purely character movement.

8 *Adage* [Sarabande, slow minuet or waltz, 4 bar phrases.]

Commence in 1st, 3rd or 5th.

1. Lunge *en avant*, supporting leg remaining fully stretched, foot flat on the floor, spine straight, arm 1st. (Note the straight line from the crown of the head to back foot.)
2. Transfer weight back to supporting leg, bringing working leg to *pointe tendue devant*.
3. Raise working leg to 90°, or as high as possible, arm to 2nd.
4. Close as at beginning.

Repeat *en croix* ensuring that weight is transferred directly over the working leg and returned without any slackening of the supporting leg or spine except when moving *en arrière*. The head must lead and, with the spine, play a proper part in creating an *arabesque* line when weight returns to the supporting leg.

At a later stage and after the leg can be held at 90°, lengthen the balance:

1. *Fondu.*
2. Straighten supporting knee.
3. Rise on *demi-pointe*.
4. Close.

Use conventional *ports de bras* throughout and ensure that the head leads.

9 Preliminary exercise for *pointe* work [Slow 3/4 in 4 bar phrases.]

Commence in 1st, facing and with both hands on the *barre*.

1. Slowly rise through $\frac{1}{4}$, $\frac{1}{2}$, $\frac{3}{4}$ and, if possible, full *pointe* (particularly if wearing soft shoes, but also in unblocked shoes if the weight is fully lifted off the legs).   .
2. Slowly sink through the same positions.
   Repeat 3 times in all without bending the knees, then *demi-plié*.
   Repeat in 2nd.

Then repeat whole exercise.

21   Opening stance, Ashton's *Les Rendezvous* (Stephen Beagley)

Stance – Intermediate *Barre*

8 *Adage* [Slow waltz or minuet in 4 bar phrases.]

Commence in 5th.

1. Simultaneously *fondu* and *pointe tendue devant*, bending forwards slightly over the working leg and holding the body still. Circle leg *en fondu* to *pointe tendue derrière*.
2. Lift and stretch both body and leg into *arabesque*.
3. *Grand rond de jambe en dedans* at 90°.
4. Close 5th *sur demi-pointes* with *ports de bras*, bending backwards. Repeat in reverse with *ports de bras* forwards.

9 Further practice for *batterie* [Steady 2/4.]

Commence in 5th, facing and with both hands on the *barre*.

Relevé 5th, bend right foot up at a right angle (foot and leg fully stretched and both legs touching). Hold the leg fully stretched and foot still, open then close it behind and then in front of supporting leg. Repeat the opening and closing as before. Then replace ball of foot in 5th *demi-pointe derrière*, then *demi-plié*, ready to repeat.

N.B. It is essential that both feet work equally and that students can feel both legs together as well as the opening from thigh to heel. They must also feel that the beat crosses at the top of the legs as well as at the ankles and calves. This should ensure the holding of the turn-out.

Stance – Advanced *Barre*

8 *Adage* [Slow 6/8 in 2 bar phrases or 12/8.]

Commence in 5th.

1. Simultaneously *fondu* and *pointe tendue devant* with *ports de bras* to 5th, *rond à terre en dehors* to *pointe tendue derrière* and lift to *arabesque*, with head fairly low.
2. *Grand rond en dedans*, rotate to *arabesque* at 90°, *coupé* into *grand rond en dehors*, *retiré* and *ports de bras* sideways.

9 Exercise for turn-out [6/8 – accent is on down beat as foot closes in 1st.]

Commence in 1st position facing and with both hands on the *barre*.

Keeping absolutely upright, spine fully stretched, head erect, pelvis steady (ensure that it does not twist), execute 8 *grands battements à la 2nde* with alternate legs as high as possible, pressing the working foot into and out of the floor to give correct impetus to the throw of the leg, but keeping the supporting leg perpendicular.

Repeat but simultaneously sink *en fondu* and lift the working leg to a very open *retiré à la 2nde*. Ensure that both legs are fully stretched when they return to 1st position.

Stance – Elementary Centre

1 (*Petit adage*) Introducing the classical walk [March on 2 bar phrases.]

Commence in 1st position *de face*.

    (1-2) *Pas marché en avant* with the right foot and opening left arm through 1st to 2nd. (3-4) Repeat using the left foot and the right arm.

    (1-2) Draw right foot to left, *bras bas*, and rise, raising arms to 5th. (3-4) Lower heels and raise opening arms to 2nd, before lowering to *bras bas* as the heels sink again.

Repeat commencing with the left foot. Repeat twice in all. Also repeat moving backwards.

Later repeat raising working leg on second step to 45° (later 90°), *tombé* forwards, transfer weight backwards, raising the same leg to 45° and close.

2 (*Petit adage*) [Waltz in 4 bar phrases.]

Commence in 5th *croisé de face*.

1. 2 *ronds à terre en dehors*, finishing *pointe tendue devant*, pass through 1st to *pointe tendue derrière* and again *devant*, close 5th.
2. Repeat using back foot and moving *en dedans*.
3. *Glissades derrière* and *devant*, *retiré passé* to change *épaulement*.
4. *Glissades en avant* and *en arrière*, rise in 5th, ready to repeat on the other side.

3 (*Grand adage*) *ADAGE* [Slow minuet in 4 bar phrases.]

Commence in 5th *de face*.

1. *Développé à la 2nde*.
2. Turn to 1st *arabesque*.
3. *Retiré*, slightly turning *effacé* into *développé effacé devant*.
4. Rise and close 5th *devant*.

Arms move through 1st to 2nd, straighten to *arabesque*, then move to 1st and open 4th to *bras bas*.

Repeat on the other side, then repeat whole exercise again. Later repeat in reverse.

Stance – Intermediate Centre

1 (*Petit adage*) [4/4 in 2 bar phrases.]

Commence in 5th *croisé*.

1. 2 *battements tendus à la 2nde*, closing 5th *derrière* and *devant*; low *développé* into *pas marché en avant sur les pointes*, closing 5th.
2. Lower heels and repeat in reverse.
3. 1 set *battements glissés en croix*.
4. *Glissé devant* into small 4th as preparation for *pirouette en dehors*, changing *épaulement* ready to repeat on the other side.

N.B. for *pirouette* pick up back foot and finish 5th *devant*.

2 (*Petit adage*) [Waltz in 4 bar phrases.]

Commence in 5th *croisé*.

1. Simultaneously *fondu* and *pointe tendue devant, rond en dehors* to *pointe tendue derrière*, stretching the supporting knee; pass leg through 1st to *grand battement devant*, closing 5th.
2. Repeat *en dedans* using back foot.
3. *Tendue devant* making a quarter turn *en dehors* to next corner, closing 5th *devant; tendue à la 2nde* making a half turn to front corner, closing 5th *derrière*.
4. Prepare into small 4th for *pirouette en dehors*, ready to repeat on the other side.

3 (*Grand adage*) *ADAGE* [Sarabande, minuet or slow waltz in 4 bar phrases.]

Commence with the right foot *pointe tendue croisé devant*.

1. 3 *pas marchés en avant* and, on the third, left foot *retiré* and *développé écarté derrière*.
2. Circle *devant* at 90°, pass through 1st to 3rd *arabesque*.
3. *Fondu* into *pas de bourrée en tournant en dehors*, finishing 5th and *développé devant* at 90°
   Grand rond de jambe en dehors, finishing 1st *arabesque*, hold. Repeat on the other side.

Stance – Advanced Centre

1 (*Petit adage*) [2/4 in 4 bar phrases.]

Commence in 5th *croisé*.

1. Full *plié*, ascend to *demi-plié* and *pirouette en dehors*, picking up back foot and finish 5th *derrière*.
2. 2 *glissés devant*, second finishing *demi-plié, chassé en avant*, closing 5th, 2 *glissés à la 2nde* and *détourné en dehors*, ready to repeat on the other side.

2 (*Petit adage*) [Waltz in 4 bar phrases.]

Commence in 5th *croisé*.

1. 2 *ronds de jambe à terre en dehors*, finishing *pointe tendue derrière*, pass through 1st into *grand battement devant*, closing 5th.
2. Repeat using back foot *en dedans*.
3. *Glissade derrière* into *relevé*, with *battement* into *petits ronds de jambe en l'air*. Repeat on the other side.
4. *Relevé retiré passé* into *pirouette en dehors*, ready to repeat on the other side.

3 (*Grand adage*) *ADAGE* [Pavane in 2 bar phrases.]

Commence *pointe tendue croisé derrière*.

1. 2 *pas marchés en avant* and on the third, step into 1st *arabesque en fondu, cabriole derrière* and pass through 1st into small 4th *croisé, relevé*. Lower heels.
2. *Relevé* making a half turn and *fondu* to *pointe tendue croisé devant*, arms 3rd as if bowing over leg.
3. Lift *devant* to 90° stretching supporting leg, circle *écarté* and close 5th *derrière*.
4. Immediately raise to *arabesque penchée*, hold. Recover and pass through 1st, transfer weight and stretch to *pointe tendue derrière*, ready to repeat on the other side.

4 Introduction to the uses of the head

1. The focus in *pirouettes* [4/4.]

Commence *de face* in 1st.

Focus on a front or 'spot' and turn the eyes slowly to the right as far as possible, without moving the head. As soon as it is no longer possible to keep the eyes fully focused on the one 'spot', turn the head directly towards the same 'spot' over the leading shoulder and complete the turn with the feet. Repeat this exercise turning to the left.

Repeat the whole exercise as often as required, ensuring that the head moves FREELY and directly from right to left or vice versa. The shoulders must be kept still.

2. The focus of the eyes to find or anticipate direction [2/4 in 2 bar phrases.]

Commence *de face* in 3rd or 5th.

(1-2) 2 *changements*. (3) Hold *demi-plié*, turning head over the right shoulder. (4) *Changement*, making quarter turn to the right.

Repeat 4 times in all, thus making one full turn.

Repeat turning to the left.

Repeat the whole exercise as often as required – and then attempt with half turns.

N.B. Ensure that the head turns directly over the appropriate shoulder and is kept focusing on the new 'spot' as the turn is made. This type of focusing must be used so that the direction to be taken has been anticipated by the head.

5 (*Petit allegro*) Introducing *glissades* and *assemblés* in squares to establish spacing as well as direction [6/8 in 2 bar phrases to establish flow of movement.]

Commence in 5th *de face*.

1. *Glissade, assemblé en avant, bras bas* to *demi-seconde; glissade, assemblé devant,* arm low 3rd to *demi-seconde*.
2. *Glissade, assemblé en arrière*, arms 1st; *glissade derrière, assemblé dessus*, arms to *demi-seconde*.

Repeat commencing with the other foot. Repeat whole exercise twice.

22 Opening *arabesque* from *La Bayadère* (Ravenna Tucker)

Stance – Intermediate Centre

4 *Pirouettes en croix* [4/4 or 3/4 with strong beats.]

Commence in 5th *de face*.

Each *pirouette en dehors* commences from an open position and finishes 5th *derrière*. It demands exact placing with correct stance and *ports de bras*.

1. *Pointe tendue devant* into small 4th *demi-plié* and *pirouette en dehors*, picking up the front foot. Finish 5th *derrière*.
2. Repeat commencing *à la 2nde*.
3. Repeat commencing small 4th *derrière*.
4. *Relevé* 5th, *demi-plié* and *pirouette en dehors*, arms 5th, finishing 5th *derrière*, ready to repeat on the other side.

N.B. This exercise is useful to establish the simple rule that *pirouettes en dehors* during the early stages of training usually finish 5th *derrière*, but those *en dedans* usually finish 5th *devant*. Such finishes help to maintain turn-out.

5 (*Petit allegro*) [Polka, 2 bar phrases.]

Commence in 5th *de face*.

1. 2 *petits jetés dessus, coupé derrière, petit assemblé*.
2. *Entrechat trois derrière, petit assemblé derrière, assemblé dessus*, ready to repeat on the other side. Arms are *demi-bras*, changing to 3rd on *entrechat trois* and opening to 2nd on the last *assemblé*.

Stance – Advanced Centre

4 *Pirouettes* with *pas de bourrée* [6/8 in 2 bar, or 3/4 in 4 bar phrases. Commence on anacrusis.]

1. (and-a-1, and-a-2) *Pas de bourrée croisé en avant* and *en arrière*.
   (and-3, and-4) Preparation for *pirouette en dedans* using *fouetté* and finishing *pointe tendue devant*.
2. (and-a-1) *Relevé* with 2 *battements battus* on front of supporting leg.
   (and-a-2) Repeat *relevé*, etc.
3. *Relevé retiré passé* to small 4th into
4. *Pirouette en dehors*, arms 5th, finishing 5th *derrière*, ready to repeat on the other side.

5 (*Petit allegro*) *Batterie* [Very steady polka in 2 bar phrases.]

Commence in 5th.

1. *Entrechat trois derrière, coupé, assemblé en avant, entrechat six*.
2. 3 *brisés dessus, changement battu*, ready to repeat on the other side.

6 (*Petit allegro*) Glissades, *assemblés* and *changements* with quarter turns [Tarantella or 2/4 in 2 bar phrases.]

Commence *de face* in 3rd or 5th.

Glissade derrière, *assemblé derrière*, 2 *changements* making a quarter turn on the second. Repeat 4 times in all to return *de face* before repeating on the other side.

Turn *en dehors*, i.e. towards the back foot. Ensure that the head is *de face* on the first and turns right in the *demi-plié* after the second, to be ready to focus on the 'spot' for the second *changement*.

Repeat 4 times in all and – when the exercise has been mastered – repeat with half turns.

7 (*Grand allegro*) Chassés to introduce gliding movements on the surface moving *en diagonale* [Waltz.]

Commence in 1st, 3rd or 5th *effacé* to audience but *de face* to corner. It is essential to help students understand this placing.

A series of *chassés en avant* across the studio. The weight of the body must be directed over the front foot as it moves forwards, the feet passing through 1st as the legs straighten. The leading foot presses easily into the floor as the dancer travels.

Once this is mastered, it is valuable to attempt a turn on the leading foot every third *chassé*, i.e. *chassés* on the right and left feet, then on the next *chassé* with the right foot give extra impetus as a preparation for a turn on the right foot. (The right arm helps to guide the shoulder round as the turn is completed.) Press forwards with another *chassé* on the left foot. And so on.

When the exercise is danced slowly without turns, it is useful to have the arms in 3rd position on each *chassé*, thus moving arms from side to side. But when danced fast, hold the arms in 3rd or 2nd. For turning, the usual preparatory 3rd should be held throughout, the outstretched arm closing in 1st for the turn.

Stance – Intermediate Centre

6 (*Petit allegro*) *Sissonnes fermées* [6/8 in 2 bar phrases.]

Commence in 5th *de face*.

Sissonne dessus, sissonne dessous, sissonne en avant, changement.

Repeat on the other side. Then repeat in reverse.

N.B. The arms should be in 3rd, the arm bent over foot coming in front and moving to 2nd during the forward movement.

7 (*Grand allegro*) [Slow waltz in 4 bar phrases.]

Commence in 5th *croisé*.

1. *Sissonne ordinaire* into *chassé, coupé, assemblé porté en avant, 2 sissonnes fermées dessus.*
2. *Glissade derrière, assemblé battu dessus, glissade derrière, assemblé derrière,* ready to repeat on the other side.

Stance – Advanced Centre

6 (*Petit allegro*) [6/8 very steady in 2 bar phrases.]

Commence *de face*.

1. 2 *échappés battus* (beat on opening and closing).
2. *Echappé croisé* into 4th, *temps levé retiré devant* into 2 *emboîtés* (i.e. 4 tiny *jetés*), ready to repeat on the other side.

7 (*Grand allegro*) [2/4 steady in 2 bar phrases.]

Commence *pointe tendue effacé derrière*.

1. *Coupé* into *ballonné devant* and *jeté élancé en avant, assemblé derrière.*
2. *Pas de bourrée en arrière* into *assemblé en arrière, entrechat six,* ready to repeat on the other side.

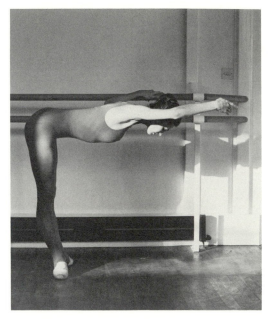

23 Practice for *ports de bras*
(Sharon McGorian):
a the hinge-like bend;

b the back bend

8 *Ports de bras*

Once past the early Elementary stage, I often add *ports de bras* and bends of the body during *pliés* at the *barre* and use them regularly in order to exercise the torso early. They remain practically the same throughout but that does not prevent variety. For example: if the *plié* is in 1st, any of the following can be used – and similarly in 2nd, 4th or 5th. Use of *ports de bras* makes students aware of the many variations of movement that are part of every lesson.

Commence in 1st, 3rd or 5th *de face* [Any slow time signature.]

1. Breathe in, stretching upwards, arms from 1st to 5th (or 2nd) whilst bending forwards to 90°, i.e. at the hip-joint. Breath should be held, spine and head kept in an absolutely straight line and the legs perpendicular. A forward stretch from the 'tail' to the crown of the head must be seen and felt. This helps to make students aware of the need to pull out the spine. Recover upright position breathing out. (See photo 23a.)

   N.B. Body and head should appear to be at a right angle to the legs.

2. Breathe in stretching upwards as arms move 1st to 5th. Bend and curl forwards in this order: head, neck (do not allow the shoulders to move) and chest. When no further movement is possible, bend downwards from the hip-joints. Recover, uncurling in the reverse order. It is essential that the head leads the body down. But it recovers its erect position when breathing out. This can only be properly performed if the shoulders do not rise and are kept well open.

3. Breathe in, arms moving to open 4th, and bend sideways away from the upraised arm. Recover and repeat other side. As in 2 above, ensure that the shoulders do not move. The upper torso bends alone by the action of the spine.

4. Breathe in, arms to 4th. Look into the upraised hand and bend backwards, leading with the head but without arching the spine. This bend is from above the waist only. (See photo 23b.)

5. A valuable circular bend should be practised in the first stages with the feet in 1st. Raise the arms to 1st, slightly bending the body forwards and turning to the right. Circle the body backwards and to the right. It should now be bending sideways again. The arms and shoulders should be kept still during this circling. Recover and repeat on the other side.

   At a later stage this circling should be taken at a greater depth, the arms moving from 4th to 3rd as the body bends forwards. Change over at the depth and return to 4th as the body circles sideways, backwards and sideways.

Stance – Intermediate Centre

8 (*Grand allegro*) [Grand waltz in 4 bar phrases.]

Commence in 5th *croisé*.

Balance *derrière* and *devant* in Russian style, i.e. spring lightly upwards from both feet, opening the leg behind into low *développé derrière*, step on to it and spring, opening front leg to low *développé devant* as preparation for 3 runs into *grand jeté croisé en avant*; repeat runs and *jeté*. *Posé devant* into 1st *arabesque* for 3 runs into *grand jeté en tournant*; *coupé* into *pirouettes enchaînées* to finish.

N.B. The direction set and the impetus given by the leg rising into *grand jeté en tournant* must be absolutely straight forwards and up. At the height of the jump both body and legs must make a clear half turn. If this is correctly performed, both legs will appear momentarily to be together in the air before weight is transferred and just before the new supporting leg descends *fondu*. In this way, students will feel how the leg giving impetus to the jump must be fully stretched as it rises and as it is held with the turn of the body if it is to arrive correctly in an *arabesque* line. In addition, the head must help the body to anticipate that line by stretching upwards and backwards as soon as the dancer turns in the air. The eyes must focus.

9 *Pirouettes enchaînées* (or *déboulés*) *en diagonale* [Gallop.]

Commence with the right foot *pointe tendue devant*, head turned over leading shoulder, eyes focused on the 'spot' in the opposite corner (see page 96).

Step directly forwards on right *demi-pointe* (or full *pointe*) making a half turn; swiftly turn head over the right shoulder and step forwards with the left foot, thus completing a full turn. Continue onwards, stepping half turn on the right foot followed by a half turn on the left foot.

N.B. The feet should be kept as close together as possible. To do this both feet should step into very small 4th. This is particularly important for girls *sur les pointes* and for both boys and girls when moving at speed. It helps to keep the legs turned out and the weight equally balanced. (See notes, pages 12 and 96.)

Stance – Advanced Centre

8 (*Grand allegro*) [Waltz in 4 bar phrases.]

Commence *pointe tendue croisé derrière*.

1. *Coupé ballonné effacé devant*, 3 runs into *grand jeté croisé en avant*, use 3rd *arabesque*.
2. Repeat on the other side.
3. *Coupé ballonné devant* and step into 2 *sauts de basque en tournant*.
4. *Coupé* and *déboulés* (or *enchaînés*) to spin off stage.

9 *Pirouettes posées* and *enchaînées* [Gallop.]

Commence *pointe tendue devant*, head turned over the leading shoulder (see page 96).

2 *posés pirouettes en dedans*, *coupé derrière* and 4 *pirouettes enchaînées*, i.e. 7 half turns on *demi-* or full *pointes*, on alternate feet. On the eighth step, *fondu derrière*, ready to repeat on the same foot.

Turn-out

PRINCIPLE

'The Turn-out must take place in the hip-joints and nowhere else.'

These three classes concentrate mostly on movements to the side and *ronds de jambe* to help students understand the degrees of rotation required. Thus to the control of the spinal muscles needed to control Stance must be added the control and use of the inner and outer thigh and buttock muscles and to some extent those in the shoulder-joints where similar degrees of rotation have to be exploited. Throughout these classes it is essential to ensure that neither hips nor shoulders twist, that legs and/or arms are rotated and that balance is maintained over one or both legs.

RULES TO FOLLOW

A   A straight line must be seen to run through the centre of the leg from hip to ankle, foot and toes whether it is bent or straight. Thus every part will be kept in proper relationship to the other. (See p.12.)

B   Whether moving from 1st or 5th (either forwards or backwards) the working foot when in *pointe tendue* must be in line with the supporting heel. This ensures that the weight is fully centred over the supporting leg. In addition, on no account must the supporting leg ever move out of the perpendicular whether the working one is circling *à terre* or *en l'air*.

FOCAL POINTS

1.   Pelvic area (see page 5).
2.   Timing movement physically (see page 15).

(see photos 24, 25a and b, 26, 27, 28, 29)

Turn-out – Elementary *Barre*

1   *Pliés* for finding depth and extent of Turn-out [Slow waltz in 2 bar phrases.]
   1.   Stand erect as in exercise 1 for Stance (page 26) feet parallel, head erect, bend knees as far as possible ensuring the 'tail' is over back of heels and knees directly in front of toes.
   2.   Turn legs outwards as far as possible without stretching knees whilst maintaining correct stance.
   3.   From this position slide one foot outwards towards 2nd, close again without stretching knees and maintaining depth of *plié*. Ensure knees are over toes and weight is fully centred.
   4.   Slide foot back to 1st and stretch knees.

N.B. At a later stage repeat moving to 4th opposite 1st *devant*, closing 1st; to 2nd closing 4th and to 4th opposite 1st *derrière*, close and stretch knees. This should be practised without stretching but maintaining depth of *plié*. Heels must be held on the floor throughout.

2   *Battements tendus* introducing rotation at the hip-joint [2/4 in 4 bar phrases or 4/4.]

Commence in 1st.

   Pointe tendue devant, turn leg inwards from hip, keeping leg fully stretched; turn leg outwards, hips must not move or knees slacken. Close.

Repeat *en croix* and repeat twice with each leg.

3   *Battements glissés* introducing difference between straight and bent legs whilst maintaining Turn-out [2/4 in 2 bar phrases.]

Commence in 1st, 3rd or 5th.
   1.   4 *glissés devant*, using right foot (preferably closing 3rd or 5th).
   2.   3 *retirés passés* using left foot and hold.

Repeat *à la 2nde* with 2 *retirés passés*. Repeat *derrière* with 3 *retirés passés* and again *à la 2nde* with 2 *retirés passés*.

N.B. It is essential that the foot movement and transfer of weight are exact. On no account allow the hips to twist.

Turn-out – Intermediate *Barre*

1 *Pliés* Repeat as for Intermediate Stance (page 26).

2 *Battements tendus* for strengthening ankles [Slow 2/4 in 2 bar phrases.]
Commence in 5th.

    1. *Pointe tendue devant*, turn foot up at a right angle without curling toes; close slowly in 5th, gradually relaxing foot on floor. Do NOT re-point toes and pull leg downwards to heel. Close 5th without allowing knees to bend.

    2. *2 tendus devant*. Close 5th (see page 6).

Repeat *derrière* and *à la 2nde* and one set *en croix*, closing 5th *demi-plié*.

N.B. Ensure weight is gradually transferred over both feet as they close and allow NEITHER KNEE to bend (see page 10).

3 *Battements glissés* [2/4 in 2 bar phrases.]
Commence in 5th.

    2 glissés devant, second closing in 5th *demi-plié*, stretch supporting leg with *glissé devant* and circle *à la 2nde*, close 5th.

Repeat whole. Then repeat with a *relevé* on supporting leg before making the circle to new point.

N.B. The circling must be exact and also the simultaneous stretch and circling without any twisting of the hips.

Turn-out – Advanced *Barre*

1 *Pliés* [5/4 in 2 bar phrases, take slowly and note beats.]
Commence in 1st position.

    1. 2 *demi-pliés*, two beats to descend and three to ascend.

    2. Full *plié*, descend for four beats pressing heels down on fifth beat and gradually rise to *demi-pointes* for five beats.

Repeat in 2nd, 4th opposite 5th and 5th, using very quick *pointe tendue* to change position.

2 *Battements tendus* [6/8 in 2 bar phrases marking beats 1 and 3, 4 and 6.]
Commence in 5th.

    (1) *Pointe tendue devant*, (3) drop heel. (4) re-point toes and circle *à la 2nde*. (6) drop heel.

Repeat above, circling from *à la 2nde* to *derriére*, close 5th and one quick *tendu derrière*. Repeat *en dedans*. Then repeat dropping into *demi-pliés* in all open positions.

3 *Battements glissés* to increase speed and accuracy [Steady 2/4 in 2 bar phrases.]
Commence in 5th.

    (and-1, and-2) 2 *glissés devant*, second closing *demi-plié*. (and-3, and-4) *Relevé* with *battement glissé devant*, lower to *pointe piquée*, *relevé* circling *à la 2nde*, close 5th *devant*.

Repeat, moving *à la 2nde* to *derrière* and in reverse.

24 *A la seconde*, from the Bluebirds' *pas de deux*, *The Sleeping Beauty* (Ravenna Tucker and Phillip Broomhead)

4 *Ronds de jambe à terre* as preparation for *assemblés soutenus* [Slow 3/4 in 4 bar or 6/8 in 2 bar phrases.]

Commence in 1st, 3rd or 5th.

1. Simultaneously *fondu* and *pointe tendue devant*, circle *à la 2nde*, straightening supporting leg and close 3rd or 5th *derrière*.
2. Repeat *en dedans*, closing 3rd or 5th *devant*.

Repeat completing one full *rond* before closing and then *en dedans*.

Repeat whole.

N.B. The arm must be used very carefully and be co-ordinated with the foot. The usual movement is from 1st to 2nd and *bras bas*, but when moving *en dedans*, use the reverse from *bras bas* to 2nd and 1st. Once mastered, students should attempt *assemblés soutenus* commencing with a simultaneous *fondu* and *pointe tendue à la 2nde*, circling *devant* whilst straightening supporting leg and closing 5th *devant*, following with a *rond en dehors* closing 5th *derrière*, then repeating in reverse. The above arm must be used when this is practised.

5 *Grands battements* introducing rotation in the hip-joint at 45° or 90° [4/4 in 2 bar phrases.]

Commence in 1st, 3rd or 5th.

Retiré, turn leg inwards until knee is directly in front of hip-joint. Turn it out holding *retiré* very firmly, close. 2 *grands battements devant*. Repeat *en croix*.

N.B. Ensure that the hips do not twist, that the weight is off the supporting leg, that the upper torso is well placed and that the working foot closes firmly, with knee fully stretched, each time it reaches the floor. Ensure that weight is now on both feet.

6 *Battements frappés* introducing a free circling of the working leg. [Slow 3/4 or tango in 4 bar phrases.]

Commence *sur le cou de pied devant*.

4 *battements frappés devant*, the accent strongly outwards, with the fourth finishing *pointe tendue devant en fondu*. Holding *fondu*, circle working leg *derrière*, *devant*, *derrière*, straighten supporting leg and prepare *sur le cou de pied* to repeat in reverse.

Repeat whole.

N.B. Ensure that the weight is maintained over the supporting leg as the other circles to and fro – and that the hips do not twist.

Turn-out – Intermediate *Barre*

4 *Ronds de jambe* with *ronds en attitude* [Slow waltz in 4 bar phrases.]

Commence in 5th.

 2 *ronds à terre en dehors*, then pass through 1st raising leg to *attitude devant* at 45° and circle *derrière* to *attitude* at 45°. Hold *attitude* momentarily and stretch into low *arabesque*.

Repeat 3 times in all, before passing leg through 1st and raise *devant* to 45°, fully stretch leg and move into *grand rond de jambe en dehors*. Close 5th *derrière*. Repeat *en dedans*.

Use same *ports de bras* as for Ex.4 (see page 28).

5 *Grands battements en croix* [4/4 in 2 bar phrases.]

Commence in 5th.

 2 *grands battements* at 90°, accent up on first beat, arms 5th, and a third *battement* opening through *développé devant* (see page 8).

Repeat *en croix*, arms 5th when *à la 2nde*, and in 2nd *arabesque*.

Repeat *sur les demi-pointes*, and later full *pointes*.

6 *Battements frappés* and *fouettés* for *pirouettes* [Strong 2/4 in 2 bar phrases.]

Commence *sur le cou de pied*.

 2 *frappés devant* at 45°, a third *frappé* finishing out *en fondu*, circle *à la 2nde* and immediately *relevé-retiré*.

Repeat *en dedans*.

Repeat whole at least twice.

Later repeat with *relevé-retiré* into *pirouette* either *en dehors* or *en dedans*, ensuring that each turn begins with the whip into *retiré*.

N.B. Ensure that the working leg circles *à la 2nde* with the supporting one *en fondu*; the *relevé* and the whip into *retiré* must be simultaneous and the head must anticipate the turn.

Turn-out – Advanced *Barre*

4 *Ronds de jambe* with *grands ronds jetés* [Slow waltz in 4 bar phrases.]

Commence in 5th.

 2 *ronds en dehors à terre*, then bring leg through 1st to *retiré devant* toe to centre front, mid-calf level; throw leg *à la 2nde* at 90° straightening supporting leg and raising arm from 3rd to 5th. Now lower leg in diagonal line to *pointe tendue derrière*, arm to open 5th.

Repeat 4 times in all. Then repeat whole *en dedans*.

N.B. Ensure that the head is correctly used, that the eyes focus on the hand as it opens in 5th. When reversing, also reverse the arm movement so that the arm falls when the leg is at the side and then into an *arabesque* line as the leg drops to *pointe tendue devant*.

Whether moving *en dehors* or *en dedans* the hips must not twist nor the arm displace the shoulder.

5 *Grands battements* with *demi-grands ronds de jambe* [4/4 in 2 bar phrases.]

Commence in 5th.

 2 *grands battements devant* at 90°, arms 5th, and a third circling *à la 2nde*, dropping arm to 2nd.

Repeat, circling from *à la 2nde* – *derrière* and in reverse.

Repeat whole *sur demi-* or full *pointe*.

6 *Retirés passés* and *petits battements* to neaten footwork [2/4 in 2 bar phrases.]

 2 *retirés passés*, fully stretched foot to reach mid-calf. Snatch foot *sur le cou de pied devant* (see page 30), 2 *petits battements*, re-point foot and *retiré passé derrière*.

Repeat in reverse. Then repeat with *retiré passé* on *relevés*, changing the *épaulement* either *croisé* or *effacé* with final *retiré*. Keep arms very simple.

25 *A la seconde* (Stephen Sherriff): *a full plié; b grand échappé*

Turn-out – Elementary *Barre*

7 *Petits battements* (See No.7 in Stance page 30 but quicken the beats.) **[2/4 in 2 bar phrases.]**

(and-1, and-2) Beat *derrière – devant* twice. (1-2) close 3rd or 5th *devant, retiré passé* to *sur le cou de pied.*

Repeat in reverse and repeat with *relevé retiré passé.*

N.B. Ensure that there is a clear movement of the foot between *sur le cou de pied* and the fully stretched foot in *retiré.*

8 *Adage* **[Slow 3/4 in 4 bar or 6/8 in 2 bar phrases.]**

Commence in 1st, 3rd or 5th.

Stretch to *pointe tendue devant*, raise to 45° (later 90°), arm to 1st and rising to 5th. Hold. Close.

Repeat *à la 2nde* opening arm through 1st to 2nd. Repeat *derrière* raising arm through 1st to 5th and then dropping to *arabesque. Ports de bras* forwards, i.e. raise arm to 5th and slowly curl body forwards dropping arm to *bras bas* and lifting it again to 5th when stretching upwards. There must be co-ordination.

Repeat in reverse, bending backwards in final *port de bras.*

9 Preparation for *pointe*-work, *échappés* and *relevés* **[Slow 3/4.]**

Commence in 5th, facing and with both hands on *barre*

Snatch feet together in 5th *relevé*, pulling inside thigh muscles together, stretching knees fully and holding weight upwards from waist. Head must be erect, shoulders relaxed. Hold position then lower to 5th *demi-plié*. Now lightly spring feet outwards, leg fully stretched to 2nd position (*échappé, sur les pointes*). Hold, then lightly spring feet together, lowering to 5th *demi-plié*.

Repeat 8 times in all, changing the feet with each closing.

N.B. The spring to open the feet must be very light, neat and small, the tips of the toes only just leaving the floor. The hold in position must be very firm and as soon as possible allow the students to take the hands off the *barre* momentarily to ensure they feel the need to balance through the whole foot and leg.

Turn-out – Intermediate *Barre*

7 *Petits battements* with *temps levé* [2/4 in 2 bar phrases.]

Commence *sur le cou de pied*.

3 *petits battements*, third finishing *en fondu*; *temps levé* raising working leg into *retiré-passé*, being sure to stretch toe fully and to raise working leg slightly. Keep arms *bras bas*.

Repeat in reverse. Repeat four times in all holding hips and shoulders facing same plane and level with each other. But use the head appropriately (see page 96), keep the arms *bras bas*.

Later repeat, changing the *épaulement* during the *temps levé*.

8 *Adage* with *tombés* [Sarabande in 2 bar phrases.]

Commence in 5th.

1. *Développé à la 2nde* at 90°, *tombé* into *ports de bras* away from *barre*. (Supporting foot must remain flat on floor, leg fully stretched. Arms move from 2nd to closed 4th.)
2. Recover *à la 2nde* at 90° and circle to *attitude*.
3. Stretch into *arabesque* and *grand rond en dedans* at 90°.
4. *Tombé en avant* into *arabesque penchée*.

Repeat in reverse.

9 Exercise for *fouettés*, *sautés* and *relevés* [Slow 2/4 or 6/8 in 2 bar phrases.]

Commence with left hand on *barre*, right leg *pointe tendue derrière*.

Swing leg through 1st to *devant* at 90° and back to *arabesque*, arm 2nd. Giving extra impetus from brief *fondu*, pass and rise through 1st to *devant* at 90° raising arm to 5th and making a clear half turn to *arabesque fondue* (see page 7).

Place right hand on *barre* and repeat above, using same leg (i.e. the one nearer the *barre*).

Repeat whole four times.

N.B. Student must be seen to be erect when at 90° *devant*, both arms 5th and then to make a clear half turn into *arabesque*. This can only be done if the raised leg is stretched away from the body at the moment of the turn and if the spine and head anticipate the stretch and curve necessary to hold an *arabesque* on completing the movement.

At a later stage this must be practised in reverse.

Turn-out – Advanced *Barre*

7 *Petits ronds de jambe en l'air* with *pirouettes fouettées* [Waltz in 4 bar phrases.]

1. Raise leg *à la 2nde* at 45° (or higher but the height must be held). 3 *petits ronds en l'air en dehors*.
2. *Fondu* into *retiré* and *développé devant*, arm to 1st, circle leg *à la 2nde*, *relevé* and simultaneously *retiré* into *pirouette en dehors*.

Repeat *en dedans*.

N.B. The timing of the *pirouette* must be accurate, i.e. at the moment of the *relevé* the working leg must have whipped from front to side and into *retiré* and turn. Ensure that eyes focus on a 'spot' or front.

8 *Adage* [Sarabande or minuet in 4 bar phrases.]

Commence in 5th.

1. *Développé à la 2nde*, circle *devant en fondu* and pass through 1st to *arabesque penchée*, recover and *retiré*.
2. *Développé à la 2nde*, rotate to *arabesque* (i.e. facing *barre*), rise and *voyagé* holding *arabesque*. Close 5th, ready to repeat on other side.

9 Stretching exercise for Turn-out [Waltz in 4 bar phrases.]

Commence by placing supporting leg at right angles to *barre* and fully stretched working leg forwards on top of *barre*. If it is correctly placed it will be slightly over-crossed. Care must be taken to see that the hips remain as square as possible to the true front as the purpose of the exercise is to stretch the upper thigh and spinal muscles behind the leg and pelvis. Arm 2nd.

1. Slowly *fondu* and stretch working leg twice without allowing working leg to move, i.e. the *fondu* is up and down, hips still, head and spine fully erect.
2. Take working leg off *barre* without losing height and correct placing so that the working toe is in line with the supporting heel. Pass through 1st to *arabesque*, arms still in 2nd.

Ensure hips and shoulders do not twist and the relationship between the legs does not change. *Fondu* and hold resultant *arabesque*.

Repeat 4 times in all and on other side.

Turn-out – Elementary Centre

1 (*Petit adage*) [4/4 in 2 bar phrases.]

Commence in 5th *croisé*.

1. *Pointe tendue devant*, drop heel and circle *à la 2nde*; drop and raise heel, circle *derrière*, drop and raise heel, close 5th *derrière*.

2. 2 *battements tendus à la 2nde* closing *derrière – devant*. Repeat using other foot. 2 *relevés retirés passés* and change *épaulement* ready to repeat on other side.

2 (*Petit adage*) [Waltz in 4 bar or 6/8 in 2 bar phrases.]

Commence in 5th *croisé*.

1. Simultaneously *fondu* and *pointe tendue devant, rond en dehors* stretching supporting knee and pivoting to come *de face* to *pointe tendue derrière*, pass through 1st to *pointe tendue devant* and again to *pointe tendue derrière*.

2. Repeat 1, and close 5th *derrière* having come *croisé* to opposite corner.

3. 4 *ronds en dedans* closing 5th *devant*.

4. *Fondu* and *pointe tendue à la 2nde* into *pas de bourrée dessous*. Repeat *pointe tendue à la 2nde* (using other foot) and *pas de bourrée dessous*. Ready to repeat on other side.

N.B. *Pas de bourrée* should first be danced with fully stretched legs and later as a *pas de bourrée piqué*. (Girls only.)

3 (*Grand adage*) *ADAGE* [Waltz or mazurka in 4 bar phrases.]

Commence in 3rd or 5th *de face*.

1. Simultaneously *fondu* and *pointe tendue à la 2nde*, circle to *pointe tendue devant*, pass through 1st stretching supporting leg and lift to *arabesque*, hold.

2. *Retiré* and *développé à la 2nde, tombé* into *pas de bourrée dessous*.

Repeat on other side and then in reverse.

26   Harlequin is born from an egg, from Fokine's *Carnaval* (Stephen Sherriff)

Turn-out – Intermediate Centre

1 (*Petit adage*) [Waltz in 2 bar phrases.]

Commence in 5th *croisé*.

1. *Glissade derrière* into left *pointe tendue à la 2nde*, arms in open 4th and stretch away from pointed toe, close 5th *devant*.
2. Repeat on other side.
3. 1 set *battements tendus en croix*.
4. Prepare with quarter *rond* to small 4th and *pirouette en dehors*, ready to repeat on other side.

2 (*Petit adage*) [6/8 in 2 bar phrases.]

Commence in 5th *croisé*.

1. *Glissade en avant sur les demi-pointes* into 5th *demi-plié* as preparation for *pirouette en dehors*, finishing *pointe tendue derrière*.
2. 3 *ronds de jambe à terre en dedans* finishing *pointe tendue devant*, drop heel as preparation for *pirouette en dedans*, finishing 5th *derrière* ready to repeat on other side.

N.B. This *pirouette en dedans* is without a *fouetté* (see page 76).

3 (*Grand adage*) ADAGE [Slow 4/4 in 2 bar or minuet in 4 bar phrases.]

Commence in 5th *croisé*.

1. Left *pointe tendue à la 2nde en fondu, rond en dedans* to *pointe tendue devant*, stretch right knee and raise left leg slowly to 90° *devant*, arms to 5th.
2. Sweep leg through 1st to *arabesque*, arms 2nd; *retiré* and *développé écarté derrière, fondu* into *pas de bourrée dessous* finishing in small 4th as preparation for *pirouette en dehors*, arms 5th, finishing *attitude croisée*.
3. *Voyagé* one full turn towards raised foot and stretch into *arabesque*.
4. Lower to *pointe tendue derrière* and *grand port de bras*.

Turn-out – Advanced Centre

1 (*Petit adage*) *Temps lié* [Slow 6/8 in 2 bar phrases, *pirouette* begins on anacrusis.]

Commence in 5th *croisé*, arms 3rd.

1. *Pirouette en dehors* (pick up front foot), move into large *chassé en avant* closing 5th *derrière demi-plié*, arms 4th stretch knees and into *ports de bras devant* (see page 40).
2. 2 *battements tendus devant* and 2 *derrière*, second closing 5th *demi-plié* into *pirouette en dehors*.
3. Large *chassé* sideways into *pointe tendue à la 2nde* arms 4th, and *ports de bras* sideways, close 5th *devant*.
4. 1 set *battements glissés en croix*, finishing 5th *devant demi-plié*, ready to repeat whole on other side.

2 (*Petit adage*) Practice for *grands ronds de jambe jetés* [6/8 in 2 bar or waltz in 4 bar phrases. Accent must be on 1st beat.]

Commence in 5th *croisé*.

1. 2 *ronds à terre en dehors*, arms 3rd, a third *rond* into *pointe tendue devant en fondu*, stretch supporting leg and throw working leg up sideways to 90°, then circle it down to *pointe tendue derrière en fondu*, arm moving from 1st to 5th and open 5th.
2. *Pas marché en arrière* and close 5th *sur demi-pointes*.

Repeat whole *en dedans* and finish *détourné* to repeat on other side.

3 (*Grand adage*) ADAGE [Slow 6/8, or 3/4, in 2 bar phrases.]

Commence in 5th *croisé*.

1. Slow *pas de basque en avant* finishing 5th *croisé* opposite corner and lift to *attitude croisée*.
2. Stretch to 3rd *arabesque fondue* into *grand fouetté relevé*.
3. Repeat *fouetté relevé* and drop to *pointe tendue derrière* and *port de bras*.
4. Transfer weight to back foot, *fondu* and bow forwards over *pointe tendue devant*, ready to repeat on other side.

4 Practice for *pirouettes* [4/4 and keep strict time.]

Commence in 3rd or 5th *de face*.

Pointe tendue à la 2nde, arms 1st, circle to *pointe tendue derrière* arms to 2nd; drop into small 4th *demi-plié*, arms 3rd. *Retiré rélevé* picking up back foot and closing arms 1st, and close feet 3rd or 5th *dernière*.

Repeat on other foot and 8 times in all.

N.B. Ensure that hips and shoulders face the same plane, the impetus for the turn is given from the back foot pushing into and out of the floor directly into *retiré*. There must also be pressure on the front foot to give the supporting leg enough impetus to stretch upwards to *demi-pointe*. The arms must NOT be thrown too far outwards and NEVER behind the shoulders.

5 (*Petit allegro*) Practice for jumps from 2 to 2 feet [2/4.]

8 jumps in 1st. 8 jumps in 2nd and 16 *changements*.

6 (*Petit allegro*) Introducing *assemblés soutenus* [Waltz in 4 bar phrases.]

Commence in 3rd or 5th *de face*.

1. *Glissade derrière, assemblé dessus; assemblé soutenu en dehors.*
2. *Glissade and assemblé en avant; assemblé soutenue en dedans.*

Repeat 4 times in all.

N.B. When mastered this should be practised with *assemblés soutenus en tournant*. The arm movements must be very simple because it is the line of the feet with its circling in contrast to the straight line of the *glissades* that is all important.

27 *Echappé sur les pointes* in fourth position, from Ashton's *Scènes de Ballet* (Julie Rose)

Turn-out – Intermediate Centre

4 *Pirouettes* with *battements frappés* [Steady tango in 4 bar phrase. Begin on anacrusis.]

Commence *sur le cou de pied*.

1. 2 *battements frappés devant*, the second immediately circling from *pointe tendue devant* to 4th *demi-plié* and *pirouette en dehors* (pick up back foot) finishing *sur le cou de pied devant*.
2. Repeat above.
3. *Relevé* with *glissé devant, tombé* into 4th as preparation for *pirouette fouetté en dedans* finishing *sur le cou de pied devant* and changing *épaulement*.
4. Repeat *relevé glissé* but into small 4th as preparation for *pirouette en dehors* finishing 5th *derrière* and *coupé* ready to repeat other side.

5 (*Petit allegro*) [Waltz in 2 bar phrases.]

Commence in 5th *de face*.

1. *Glissade derrière* into *temps levé* with *petits ronds de jambe en l'air*. Close 5th *devant*.
2. Repeat on other side.
3. *Sissonne ouverte élancé en avant, coupé assemblé en avant*.
4. *Sissonne fermée en avant, changement battu*, ready to repeat.

6 (*Petit allegro*) [2/4 in 8 or 4/4 in 4 bar phrases. Start on anacrusis.]

Commence in 5th *croisé*.

Failli (changing *épaulement*), *glissade en arrière* (i.e. come *de face* and move directly backwards); *temps de cuisse* (i.e. bring back foot forwards into 5th with quick *retiré* followed by *sissonne devant*), followed by 3 *sissonnes fermées dessous, dessus* and *dessous, entrechat quatre*, ready to repeat on other side.

Turn-out – Advanced Centre

4 Practice for and introduction to *grandes pirouettes* [4/4.]

Commence in 5th *de face*.

Pointe tendue à la 2nde, simultaneously *demi-plié* in 2nd and *relevé*, raising working leg *à la 2nde* to 90° and making a half turn. Close 5th and repeat to return *de face*.

Repeat with other foot.

Repeat twice in all.

Repeat making one complete turn.

Then repeat the following *enchaînement* 4 times in all:

Commence in 5th *croisé*. [Girls prefer 3/4 and boys 4/4.]

Relevé retiré passé to small 4th *croisé* in *demi-plié* and *pirouette en dehors* finishing *à la 2nde* at 90°. Hold position momentarily. Drop to *pointe tendue à la 2nde, demi-plié*. Simultaneously stretch and raise the working leg *à la 2nde* at 90° into *pirouette en dehors*, finishing in the same pose and holding the position *de face*.

Repeat using other leg.

5 (*Petit allegro*) [Steady polka in 2 bar phrases.]

Commence in 5th *croisé*.

1. 2 *brisés dessus, pas de basque en dehors* (*en avant*).
2. 2 *sissonnes fermées en avant, pas de basque en dedans*, ready to repeat on other side.

6 (*Petit allegro*) [6/8 in 2 bar phrases.]

Commence in 5th *de face*.

1. *Echappé battu à la 2nde* (beating both on opening and closing), 2 *brisés dessous*.
2. *Glissade derrière, assemblé derrière, assemblé battu dessus, changement, grand échappé* (i.e. jump up opening and descend into 5th *devant*, ready to repeat on other side.

28 *Echappé à la seconde,* from the Bluebirds' *pas de deux, The Sleeping Beauty* (Ravenna Tucker) – compare with photograph 21

29 *Grand échappé:* Florestan's sister from *The Sleeping Beauty* (Karen Paisey) – compare with photograph 25*b*

7 (*Petit allegro*) [2/4 in 4 bar phrases.]

Commence in 3rd or 5th *de face.*

1. *Glissade, jeté derrière, temps levé, petit assemblé derrière.* Repeat on other side.
2. *Glissade, assemblé en avant.* Repeat *en arrière.* 3 *changements* and hold ready to repeat on other side.

N.B. When mastered use changing *épaulement* on *temps levé.*

8 (*Grand allegro*) Introducing *pas de basque* [*A six temps,* i.e. 3 strong beats in 4 bar phrases.]

Commence in 3rd or 5th *croisé.*

1. *Pas de basque glissé en avant,* 3 *soubresauts* travelling slightly forwards. Keep feet tightly closed together. Repeat on other side.
2. *Pas de basque glissé en arrière, glissade – assemblé derrière.* Repeat.

Repeat 4 times in all.

N.B. It is essential to distinguish between the circling-gliding movement of the *pas de basque* and the upward jump of the *soubresauts.*

9 *Ports de bras* 'The Circles' [Waltz.]

Commence in 5th *croisé.*

From *bras bas,* with head lowered and eyes focused on hands, open the arms sideways, wrists pressing against the air, palms down until they are above the head, which has been straightened. Turn the wrists so that the arms are now in 5th. Open arms to 2nd, palms facing front and turning head towards front arm. Straighten that arm into *arabesque* line (i.e. palm down and turn body towards it). Whilst straightening the other arm, circle body to opposite side allowing hands to press against the air, but do not change the angle of the head. Return arms to 2nd, straighten head, bring arms *bras bas* and lower head as at the beginning. *Assemblé soutenu en dedans* (changing *épaulement*), ready to repeat on other side.

7 (*Grand allegro*) *Temps lié* with *assemblé porté* [Grand waltz or 6/8.]

Commence in 5th *croisé*.

Sissonne ordinaire into *chassé en avant* (directing body and arms forwards); then into 1st *arabesque* and *assemblé porté en avant* closing 5th *derrière*, arms to 3rd. Repeat moving *à la 2nde*, moving arms to 2nd and *bras bas* as feet close in 5th *devant*, ready to repeat on other side.

N.B. The tips of the toes should merely skim the surface of the floor throughout so that the *enchaînement* is *glissé* but well travelled. The arm movements must be very simple and economical.

7 (*Grand allegro*) [Tango in 4 bar phrases.]

Commence in 5th *croisé*.

2 *sissonnes fermées en avant*, turn backwards into 2 *pas marchés* and *grand jeté croisé en avant*, *assemblé derrière*, *sous-sous*, *entrechat six*. Repeat with the same foot.

8 (*Grand allegro*) *Fouettés sautés en diagonale* [Tango.]

Commence *pointe tendue croisé derrière*.

Posé en avant into 1st *arabesque* (holding momentarily), turn into two running steps and on the third spring into *fouetté sauté*, arms moving from 1st to 5th and 3rd *arabesque*. Hold *arabesque fondue* before repeating.

Repeat as many times as possible always using the same foot before changing sides.

8 (*Grand allegro*) [Grand waltz in 8 bar phrases.]

Commence *pointe tendue croisé derrière*.

Demi-contretemps into *assemblé battu dessus*; *sissonnes fermées dessus – dessous* and step into 2 *sauts de basque*, *assemblé en avant*, *temps levé*, stretching working leg to *pointe tendue derrière*, ready to repeat on other side.

9 *Pas de bourrée en tournant* [Gallop.]

Commence *de face*, head turned over leading shoulder (see page 96).

Lightly spring on right foot, making a quarter turn and simultaneously circle left foot *devant* making three quarter turn. Close right 5th *devant*, ready to repeat in series.

N.B. This can also be danced with a strong *sauté* on first step as if starting a *pas de chat*. The second and third step on *demi-* or full *pointe* will then be almost *en place*. In both versions, the arms must be well rounded and controlled with as little movement as possible.

At a later stage the second version should be practised with the arms rising to 5th and opening to 2nd with the spring on the first step.

9 *Pirouettes posées* and *tours enchaînés* [2/4 in 4 bar phrases.]

Commence *pointe tendue de face*, head turned over leading shoulder (see page 96).

2 *pirouettes posées en dedans*, *coupé* into 4 *tours enchaînés* (i.e. 7 tiny steps on *demi* or full *pointes*, making a half turn on each step and on the eighth *coupé*, ready to repeat as at beginning).

N.B. The feet should be closed in tiny 4th as weight is transferred because *enchaînés* are best practised making half a turn on each leg. (See notes, page 67 for *posés* and page 96 for *enchaînés*.)

30 Aurora moving into a *pirouette,* from *The Sleeping Beauty* (Fiona Chadwick) – compare with photographs 54*a* and 54*b*, and note the head

31 Aurora moving *élancé* (Fiona Chadwick)

Placing

PRINCIPLE

'Each part of the body must be kept in proper relationship to the other and to the central line of balance if classical dance is to retain its purest form.'

Placing in classical dance usually means how dancers relate movements to the points of the square in which they move. They can face any one of eight points. Thus when teachers first place a child at the *barre* they must immediately establish the front, or *de face*. That is the child must stand facing directly forwards so that he or she is at a right angle to the *barre*. Hence the placing of the hand is all important (page 18). This will help establish the need always to be square to a particular front, hips and shoulders facing the same plane and lying parallel to each other and the floor. From that particular front are to be found the other eight points which the body can face to achieve movements in the *croisé, effacé* and *écarté épaulements*. Exercises should be introduced to the Intermediate and Advanced stages which find the dancer moving easily from one point to another. When using such exercises, ensure that the hips and shoulders are correctly placed and square to the necessary front, so that the step or pose can be directed onwards by the proper use of the head.

But placing is also concerned with how dancers place one part of the body in relationship to another and to the whole. Thus some exercises here give more detailed descriptions for the exact placing and spacing needed to ensure how large a position or step must be taken as a preparation for a *pirouette en dehors* with a slightly larger one for a *pirouette en dedans* commencing with a *fouetté* or an even larger one for a *temps lié* or a *tombé* from 90° to a lunge (page 12).

It is important during the early stages of training that a clear distinction is made between the small and large open positions, particularly when teaching *pirouettes*. When turning *en dehors* or *en dedans* students must feel the direct upward pull and stretch on the supporting leg from *demi-* to full *pointe* the moment the turn begins. Therefore they must take the appropriate preparation. For *en dehors* from 2nd or 4th a small position is needed. For *en dedans* from 4th the preparation is best taken from *pointe tendue derrière*, weight centred over a straight supporting leg. Then simultaneously bend that knee and lower the back heel without in any way changing stance, so that the head and body remain exactly placed over the leg that will support and turn.

Throughout these three classes students must place their bodies firmly and centrally over one or both legs. The pelvic area is like a balancing board set over one or two sticks. The torso is balanced over that area and over the torso, the head – the heaviest part of the body. The legs and arms are set on each side of the central line and SHOULD NEVER CROSS IT. Thus when using alignment hips and shoulders face the same plane, parallel to each other and the floor (page 5). When using *épaulement* the hip line remains parallel to the floor, but the upper torso is slightly turned inwards or outwards from the waist, one or other shoulder possibly slightly lowered.

RULES TO FOLLOW

A The natural articulation of the leg at its joints must not be distorted.
   a. The foot bends directly upwards or downwards at the ankle in the same line as the lower leg.
   b. The lower leg only bends backwards towards the upper leg at the knee joint.
   c. The upper leg only bends backwards and upwards towards the body at the hip-joint whether turned in or out. It is, therefore, essential that the dancer tilts slightly forwards at the pelvis when moving into *arabesque* and compensates by curving the upper spine and head backwards towards the centre.

B The arms are always held away from the body and rounded except in *arabesque* (page 96).

C The floor must be used as a spring-board, and every movement when taking off and landing from a jump (page 7) must be seen to travel through the entire leg and foot from heel to toe and vice-versa.

FOCAL POINTS

1. Exact relationship of feet and legs (see pages 6, 7).
2. The arms (see page 9).
3. The head (see page 10).

(see photos 30, 31, 32, 33, 34, 35 and 36)

1 *Pliés*

Repeat as for Turn-out (page 42).

2 *Battements tendus* as an introduction to *chassé* and *pas marché* [4/4 in 2 bar phrases.]

Commence in 1st, 3rd or 5th.

2 *tendus devant*, second closing *demi-plié*; *chassé en avant* transferring weight through centre, stretch new supporting leg; working toe should not move as leg stretches to *pointe tendue derrière*. Close 5th *derrière*.

Repeat, moving *en arriére* and *à la 2nde*, moving away and towards the *barre*. These sideways movements help to stabilise and strengthen the 'muscular corset'.

3 *Battements glissés* to distinguish between a straight and bent leg when raised to 20°, thus controlling the height of the upper leg [2/4 or tarantella in 2 bar phrases.]

Commence in 1st, 3rd or 5th.

2 *glissés devant* to 20° closing 3rd or 5th (weight must be held over supporting leg), *retiré devant*, fully pointed toe should reach bottom of calf, close 5th *devant*.

Repeat *en croix* using *retiré passé* when moving from side to back.

Repeat closing second *glissé* in *demi-plié* and raising toe to centre of calf during *retiré*.

32 Aurora moving in *pointes piquées sautées,* from *The Sleeping Beauty* (Fiona Chadwick)

Placing – Intermediate *Barre*

1 *Pliés* to strengthen the 'muscular corset' [3/4 in 8 bar or 6/8 in 4 bar phrases.]

Commence in 1st.

2 rises in 1st, 1 full *plié*, 2 *demi-pliés* and 1 full *plié*, raising arm to 5th during descent and lowering it through 1st to *bras bas* during ascent, i.e. a reversed *port de bras* using head to direct the line but keeping spine erect.

Repeat in 2nd, 4th opposite 5th and 5th.

2 *Battements tendus* with placing of feet [4/4 in 2 bar phrases.]

Commence in 5th.

1. Raise heel (foot rests in front of other on *demi-pointe*), stretch foot and toes (tips now rest on floor opposite supporting heel), lower heel into 5th *devant*. Repeat, using other foot *derrière*.
2. 2 *tendus* closing 5th *devant* and 2 *tendus à la 2nde*, the second closing 5th *derrière*.

Repeat in reverse, then repeat whole, closing 1st *tendu* in 5th *demi-plié*.

3 *Battements glissés* with *pas marchés* on *demi-pointes* [2/4 in 4 or 6/8 in 2 bar phrases.]

Commence in 5th.

2 *battements glissés devant*, second closing 5th *demi-plié*. Simultaneously *relevé* and *glissé* to 20°, step forwards and close 5th *sur demi-pointes*, lower heels.

Repeat *derrière* and *à la 2nde* away and towards the *barre*.

N.B. Ensure that the hips do not twist when heel drops in open position and raise arm to 5th. Also keep weight central when stepping foot away from the *barre*. The head should anticipate throughout the direction to be taken.

Placing – Advanced *Barre*

1 *Pliés*

Repeat as for Stance (page 27).

2 Footwork into small *chassés* [4/4 in 4 bar phrases.]

Commence in 5th.

Lift heel *devant* so that metatarsal arch rests lightly on floor, stretch foot until it is fully pointed with the tips still on the floor, replace metatarsal arch, and drop heels in 5th ensuring that both knees are stretched and weight fully centred. Repeat *derrière*.

Chassé en avant merely transferring weight slightly backwards to allow working foot to slide forwards to small 4th with straight knees, rise to *demi-pointes*, lower heels, and draw feet together by merely sliding working foot backwards.

Repeat moving *à la 2nde* and closing 5th *derrière*.

Repeat moving backwards and then again *à la 2nde*.

3 *Battements glissés* with *chassés* [6/8 in 2 bar or 3/4 in 4 bar phrases.]

Commence in 5th.

2 *glissés devant*, the second finishing 5th *demi-plié*. *Chassé en avant* into *relevé* with *glissé derrière*, hold, close 5th *derrière*.

Repeat, moving *en arrière* and *à la 2nde*, away and towards the *barre*.

N.B Use head in the same way as in *battements tendus*, indicating the direction to be followed.

33 *Arabesque allongée,* from *La Bayadère* (Bryony Brind)

4 *Ronds de jambe*, defining each quarter *rond* [Slow waltz in 4 bar phrases.]

Commence in 1st, 3rd or 5th on last beat of introduction. This is essential because in each phrase the *ronds* commence at a different *pointe tendue* and must finish there.

1. 3 *ronds à terre en dehors* finishing *pointe tendue devant*, drop heel in 4th opposite 5th, raising arm to 5th. Raise heel, *bras bas* and commence *rond*.
2. 3 *ronds en dehors* finishing *pointe tendue à la 2nde*, drop heel, arm to 5th. Raise heel, *bras bas* and commence *rond*.
3. 3 *ronds en dehors* finishing *pointe tendue derrière*, drop heel, arm to 5th, then to *bras bas*.
4. Pass working foot through 1st to *pointe tendue devant* and back to *pointe tendue derrière*, close 5th, arm opens from 1st to 2nd and is held.

Repeat whole, moving *en dedans*.

5 *Grands battements* with foot action [4/4 in 2 bar phrases.]

Commence in 1st, 3rd or 5th.

Raise leg *devant* to 90°, turn foot up at ankle. Re-point toe, close. 2 *grands battements devant*.

Repeat *en croix*.

6 *Battements frappés* defining difference between *sur le cou de pied* and *retiré* [2/4 in 2 bar phrases.]

Commence *sur le cou de pied*.

1. 3 *battements frappés devant*, *petit battement* beating *devant – derrière*.
2. Repeat *derrière*, beating *derrière – devant*.
3. Repeat *à la 2nde*, close *sur le cou de pied derrière*.
4. *Relevé retiré* as high as possible.

Repeat in reverse.

N.B. A clear distinction must be made between the foot *sur le cou de pied* and in *retiré*.

Placing – Intermediate *Barre*

4 *Ronds de jambe*

Repeat as for No.4 page 29, but use *demi-plié* when heel drops in open position and raise arm to 5th with very slight bend of body towards working foot when moving *en dehors*, and backwards when moving *en dedans*. Finish by passing through 1st to *devant* at 90° and return to *arabesque*.

5 *Grands battements en croix* [4/4 in 2 bar phrases. Accent must be up on beats 1 – 3 – 5 – 7.]

Commence in 5th.

Throw leg *devant* to 90° and close 5th *demi-plié*. Repeat but close in small 4th *demi-plié*. Repeat, closing 5th *demi-plié*. Repeat but simultaneously throw leg upwards and *relevé*. Close 5th lowering both heels.

Repeat *en croix* being careful to ensure that weight is over both feet when in the open positions, with hips and shoulder square to a front.

6 *Battements frappés* with *flic-flac* [Strong 2/5 in 2 bar phrases.]

Commence *sur le cou de pied*.

1. 3 *frappés à la 2nde* and a fourth finishing *en fondu*.
2. Simultaneously *relevé* and whip working foot *devant – derrière* by brushing the pads of the toes on the floor twice with a slight opening of the leg to the side and making two half turns finishing *en fondu, pointe tendue à la 2nde*. Hold and repeat *flic-flac*.

N.B. This *flic-flac* needs flexibility of the whole foot, particularly the metatarsal arch and ankle as both must give the dancer sufficient impetus to make two half turns as the working fore foot brushes the floor. There are other versions using a fully pointed foot. But this one is needed to ensure students understand the amount of impetus that can be given to certain types of jump and turn by a proper use of the floor as a spring-board.

Placing – Advanced *Barre*

4 *Ronds de jambe* with placing [Waltz in 4 bar phrases.]

Commence in 5th.

1. 2 *ronds à terre en dehors, fondu* and *pointe tendue devant*, pass through 1st, straightening supporting leg before sinking to *pointe tendue derrière en fondu*, and repeat this transfer.
2. Repeat above.
3. 2 *ronds en dehors* finishing *en fondu*, but raise leg to 90° *devant*, arm to 5th.
4. *Retiré* stretching supporting leg, *développé en fondu* into *arabesque*, bring back to *retiré* and *développé à la 2nde*. Close 5th *derrière*.

Repeat *en dedans*.

N.B. Ensure that the supporting leg bends and stretches down and up in an absolutely perpendicular line and that the hips do not twist. The shoulders too must be kept facing front.

5 *Grands battements* [Polonaise in 8 bar phrases. Note timing.]

Commence in 5th.

(1) *Relevé* directly into *attitude devant effacée*, arm 5th. (2) Open *devant* above 90° arm to open 5th. (3) Hold.

(1) *Retiré* dropping arm to 1st. (2) Close 5th *derrière*. (3) Lower heels. Repeat, lifting to *attitude effacée* on second beat, etc.

(1) *Relevé* directly into *attitude devant*. (2) Hold. (3) Pass through *retiré* and open to (1). *Attitude*, arm to open 5th. (2) Hold. (3) Close 5th.

Repeat twice in all.

6 *Battements frappés* with double and triple beats [2/4 in 2 bar phrases.]

Commence *sur le cou de pied*.

1. 4 *frappés doublés à la 2nde*, i.e. beat *derrière – devant* before first opening, then *devant – derrière* before second opening.
2. 4 *frappès devant* with triple beats, i.e. beat *devant – derrière – devant* before each opening.

Repeat moving *à la 2nde* and *derrière*, i.e. *en croix*.

Repeat with *relevés* on each beaten section.

N.B. Ensure that hips and knees are kept still to sustain turn-out and height of *frappés*.

7 *Petits battements* as preparation for *batterie* [Slow 2/4 in 2 bar phrases.]

Commence *sur le cou de pied*.

(and-1, and-2, and-3) Beat *derrière – devant* three times, accenting *devant*. (This is equivalent to three *entrechats quatre*.) (and-4) Beat *devant – derrière*, i.e. one *changement battu*.

Repeat in reverse. Repeat whole.

8 *Adage* Slow *développés* [Slow waltz in 4 bar phrases.]

Commence in 1st, 3rd or 5th.

Développé devant at 90°, close 5th and repeat *en croix*.

N.B. When performing *développés* it is important that when the leg is raised to *retiré* the tips of the toes should all but rest on the centre front, side or back of the supporting leg. When it can rise no higher, the upper leg should be slightly raised, knee opened and then held at that height as the lower leg is extended outwards if any pose at 90° or above is to be held. The muscles responsible for lifting the leg activate the upper half only. Others must take over when extension is required.

9 Practice for *pointes* and *pas de bourrée* [3/4, dance to each beat.]

Commence facing and with both hands on the *barre*, feet parallel, toes facing front.

(1) Step (*posé*) straight on to right *pointe*, stretching fully upwards, head lifted and shoulders down (see that the inner thigh muscles are drawn together and that the waist is slimmed).(2) Step straight on to left *pointe* at side of right. (3 – 4) Lower feet through $\frac{3}{4}$, $\frac{1}{2}$ and $\frac{1}{4}$ *pointes*.

Repeat commencing with the left foot and repeat four times in all.

Now repeat turning legs outwards and using *pas de bourrée dessous* and *dessus* alternately. Ensure that legs are picked up into *retiré* and placed either behind or in front of 5th during transfer, i.e. feet should move from *retiré* to 5th, 1st and 5th.

34 *Attitude devant,* from the peasant *pas de deux, Giselle* (Karen Paisey)

Placing – Intermediate *Barre*

7 *Petits battements serrés* [2/4 in 4 bar phrases.]

Commence *sur le cou de pied*.

1. Beat *derrière* – *devant* eight times, accenting front.
2. *Relevé* turning *effacé* and opening working leg to 20°. Close fully pointed foot *devant*, resting it over instep and beat 6 times against supporting foot. (Toe should reach the ankle-bone.)
3. Repeat *petits battements*, returning *de face*.
4. *Relevé* turning *effacé*, working leg to 20°. Close pointed toe *derrière* just across mid-calf and, turning towards the *barre*, bend slightly backwards before opening the leg and circling and closing it 5th *devant*, *détourné*, ready to repeat on other side.

8 *Adage* Introducing *arabesque penchée* [Sarabande in 2 bar phrases.]

Commence in 5th.

1. *Développé à la 2nde*, close 5th *derrière* and immediately raise to *arabesque penchée*, the body well stretched downwards and the supporting leg absolutely perpendicular.
2. Recover and rotate to *devant* at 90°, arm 2nd.
3. Close 5th and *développé à la 2nde*, arm moving through *bras bas*, 1st and 2nd.
4. *Retiré* and raise leg to *attitude devant* as high as possible. Stretch leg above 90° *devant*, open arm to 5th and hold.

9 Exercise for *sissonnes fermées* or *sur les pointes* [Strong 3/4 or tango.]

Commence facing and with both hands on *barre* in 5th.

Demi-plié then simultaneously spring upwards and very slightly sideways on the right foot to the right whilst opening left *à la 2nde* to 30°. Hold the left leg in this position and descend *en fondu* before closing 5th *devant* and stretching both knees. Repeat using the other foot. Then repeat reversing and closing 5th *derrière*.

When this exercise has been mastered, repeat *en croix* both *sauté* and with *relevé sur les pointes*. In this case the spring on to the *pointes* must be small and exact, weight held well away from the waist and fully centred over the supporting leg.

N.B. Ensure that both legs leave the floor together and that the supporting leg finishes *en fondu* when using *sauté* or held *sur la pointe* when using *relevé* before the working leg closes in 5th. Only then allow the legs to stretch or sink to the floor.

Placing – Advanced *Barre*

7 *Petits battements battus* with *relevés* and *pointes tendues* [Polka, in 2 bar phrases. Note timing.]

(and-a-1) *Relevé* beating fully pointed toe against ankle twice, *fondu* and *pointe tendue éffacé devant*. (and-a-2) Repeat.

(and-a-3) *Pas de bourrée piqué devant* closing 5th *devant*, *demi-plié*.

(and-a-4) *Relevé passé derrière* turning *effacé* towards the *barre*.

Repeat moving *derrière*. Repeat whole, turning *croisé*.

N.B. Ensure that the *épaulements* used are correctly placed with the slightest twist of the upper torso towards the pointed toe or away. The exact angle can be slightly varied.

8 *Adage* [Minuet in 2 bar phrases.]

Commence in 5th *écarté*, i.e. turning towards *barre*, head turned over working shoulder.

1. *Fondu* and *développé écarté devant* and circle *devant* at 90°, i.e. dancer should now be *croisé*.
2. Pass through 1st and raise to *arabesque penchée* (see photo 40, page 74).
3. Recover to *attitude*, *fondu* into *retiré* and rotate outwards to *devant* at 90°, arms 5th.
4. *Tombé en avant* and *relevé* to *arabesque*, arms 2nd. Hold. Close 5th. Step back to *barre* and turn ready to repeat on other side.

N.B. Ensure that alignment is stable throughout, the head leading the movement to find the appropriate front. In the *tombé* see that the student follows the toe down (see page 13).

9 *Battements balançoire* [Steady 6/8, accent up, and 2 movements to each bar.]

Commence *pointe tendue derrière*.

Keeping supporting leg absolutely perpendicular throughout, arms 2nd and shoulders and hips square and as still as possible, throw working leg through 1st as high as possible *devant*, stretching head and upper torso very slightly backwards, and then swing leg backwards into *arabesque*, still holding that position. The body must be seen to be in a correct *arabesque* over the supporting leg. The swing should be repeated 16 times, the last *arabesque* held.

The exercise can also be repeated using *attitude devant* and *attitude*, in which case the working leg must be stretched downwards into 1st so that the upper leg has to be lifted straight forwards or backwards. The working foot must be seen correctly to touch the floor as it reaches and passes through 1st.

Placing – Elementary Centre

1 (*Petit adage*) [Slow waltz in 4 bar or 4/4 in 2 bar phrases.]

Commence in 5th *croisé*.

Chassé en avant on straight legs, rise, lower heels and close 5th. 2 *tendus devant*, the second closing *demi-plié*. *Chassé en avant* and close 5th *derrière*. Repeat *en arrière* and *à la 2nde*. *Glissade croisé en avant, glissade dessous*, coming *de face, glissade croisé en arrière* and rise. Repeat on other side.

N.B. Make a clear distinction between the first and second *chassé*. In the first merely release the foot and slide it just over the surface. In the second use the usual *chassé* from *demi-plié*. The first comes to a small 4th and the second to a normal 4th.

2 (*Petit adage*) [Waltz in 4 bar phrases.]

Commence in 5th *croisé*.

1. Simultaneously *fondu* and *pointe tendue devant* with *rond en dehors*, close 5th *derrière*. 2 *grands battements effacé devant*.
2. Repeat in reverse.
3. 4 *ronds à terre en dehors* to change *épaulement*, i.e. to opposite corner.
4. 3 *ronds en dedans*, closing 5th *derrière*, ready to repeat on other side.

3 (*Grand adage*) *ADAGE* [Sarabande or minuet in 4 bar phrases.]

Commence in 5th *croisé*

1. *Glissade en avant*, stretch to *pointe tendue derrière* and raise to 3rd *arabesque*, close 5th *derrière*.
2. Repeat in reverse.
3. Repeat with *glissade écarté devant*, raising to *écarté devant*, closing 5th *devant*.
4. *Chassé en avant* with sweeping *ports de bras, retiré passé* changing *épaulement* and closing 5th, ready to repeat on other side.

N.B. 'Sweeping' *ports de bras* – the arms should move from *bras bas* through 1st to slightly straightened 2nd, palms upwards during the *retiré*.

Placing – Intermediate Centre

1 (*Petit adage*) [Waltz in 4 bar phrases.]

Commence in 5th *croisé*.

    1. *Rond de jambe à terre en dehors en fondu* to *pointe tendue derrière* using opposition arms; *pas marché en arrière* closing 5th *sur demi-pointes* and *pas marché en avant* also closing *demi-pointes*.

    2. Repeat in reverse, i.e. *en dedans*.

    3. 4 *ronds en dehors*, changing *épaulement*.

    4. And a fifth *rond* as preparation for *pirouette en dehors*, closing 5th *derrière* ready to repeat on other side.

2 (*Petit adage*) [2/4 in 2 bar phrases.]

Commence standing *croisé sur le cou de pied*.

    1. 2 *battements frappés devant* and a third finishing *pointe tendue devant en fondu*, *rond en dehors* to *pointe tendue derrière* (stretching supporting knee) and snatch *sur le cou de pied derrière*.

    2. Repeat in reverse, finishing *sur le cou de pied devant*.

    3. Circle leg with 4 *pointes piquées en croix*, closing 5th *devant*.

    4. *Glissé effacé devant* to small 4th and *pirouette en dehors*, finishing with *coupé*, ready to repeat on other side.

3 (*Grand adage*) ADAGE [Sarabande in 4 bar phrases.]

Commence in 5th.

    1. Rise with arms 5th, lower heels and *demi-plié* with arms 1st, *chassé en avant* raising working leg to 3rd *arabesque*, pass through 1st and raise to 4th *devant* at 90°.

    2. Rotate to *écarté devant*, *fondu* into *pas de bourrée dessous* and small 4th, raise to *attitude*.

    3. *Voyagé* towards raised leg, making one complete turn.

    4. Bend body sideways into *pas de bourrée en tournant en dehors* and *changement*, ready to repeat on other side.

Placing – Advanced Centre

1 (*Petit adage*) [Slow 4/4 in 2 bar phrases.]

Commence in 5th *croisé*.

    1. Full *plié* in 5th, *chassé en avant* to *pointe tendue derrière*, close 5th *derrière* and 2 *battements glissés derrière*.

    2. Repeat *chassé* and *glissés en arrière*, prepare *pointe tendue derrière* to small 4th and *pirouette en dehors*, ready to repeat on other side.

2 (*Petit adage*) [Polonaise in 2 bar phrases, use same timing as No.5, page 59, in *Barre*-work.]

Commence in 5th *croisé*.

    1. *Relevé attitude devant*, stretch and hold; drop to *pointe tendue devant*, 2 *ronds en dehors*, closing 5th *derrière*.

    2. Repeat with *relevé* into *attitude effacée*, stretch and hold; drop to *pointe tendue derrière* and *assemblé soutenu en tournant en dehors*, ready to repeat on other side.

Repeat in reverse using *croisé épaulement*.

3 (*Grand adage*) ADAGE [Slow minuet in 2 bar phrases.]

Commence in 5th *croisé*.

    1. *Pas de basque* into 5th *croisé*, arms 4th and into small circular *ports de bras* (see page 40) and note same arm up as foot in front).

    2. *Développé devant* and rotate through *écarté* to 3rd *arabesque*.

    3. Pass through 1st to *devant* at 90° and rotate to 1st *arabesque*.

    4. *Relevé* and pass through 1st to 4th *croisé* for *pirouette en dedans*, arms 5th and finishing 5th *devant*. *Relevé* and change to *à deux bras*. Repeat on other side.

4 Repeat exercise for *pirouettes* on page 50 but use turns.

It is important that students realise the impetus given by the drive into and out of the floor by both feet as well as the intake of breath as the turn begins and the exact focusing and movement of the eyes and head. Another important factor is the pressure put behind the shoulder coming into the turn. For all these reasons it is useful to practise *en dehors pirouettes* in three different ways to establish Stance, Turn-out and Placing.

1. With hands placed firmly on the hips throughout and making one turn with the impetus from the feet, head and breath.
2. With right hand on hip and left arm preparing in 2nd, but quickly moving to shortened 1st (or vice-versa when turning to the left), make two turns, extra impetus being given by the shoulder coming into the turn. Do NOT ALLOW the incoming arm to go behind the shoulder, nor to over-cross the centre. This movement should be FELT by the dancer, and not seen.
3. With usual *pirouette* arms, make three or more turns.
   DO NOT USE ALTERNATE FEET during the sequence.

5 (*Petit allegro*) [2/4 in 2 bar phrases.]
Commence in 3rd or 5th *de face*.
1. *Assemblé en avant, 2 petits jetés derrière, coupé.*
2. *Assemblé en avant, sissonne ordinaire à la 2nde, pas de bourrée dessous, entrechat quatre*, ready to repeat on other side.
This should also be danced in reverse.

6 (*Petit allegro*) Practice for *echappés sautés* in 2nd and 4th [2/4 in 2 bar phrases.]
1. 2 *échappés fermés* in 2nd, closing 3rd or 5th and changing feet on each closing.
2. *Echappé fermé* into 4th *croisé, changement* ready to repeat on other side.
Repeat 4 times in all.

35   Sword play, from MacMillan's *Romeo and Juliet* (Michael Batchelor)

Placing – Intermediate Centre

4 *Pirouettes* [2/4 in 2 bar phrases.]

Commence in 5th *de face*, *effacé* or *croisé*. (All should be tried.)

1. 2 *glissés devant*, the second closing 5th *demi-plié* as preparation for *pirouette en dehors* (pick up front foot), finishing 5th *derrière*.
2. Repeat *derrière*, picking up same foot.
3. Repeat *à la 2nde*, still picking up same foot and finishing 5th *devant*.
4. *Glissé devant* into 4th as preparation for *pirouette en dedans* (with *fouetté*) finishing 5th *devant*, ready to repeat on other side.

5 (*Petit allegro*) [Steady 2/4 in 2 bar phrases.]

Commence in 5th *de face*.

1. 2 *petits jetés derrière*, *petit assemblé* and *temps levé derrière*.
2. Turning *effacé*, *pas de bourrée en avant*, *pas de bourrée en arrière* and *en tournant en dedans*, *changement*, ready to repeat on other side.

6 (*Petit allegro*) [6/8 in 2 bar phrases.]

Commence in 5th *croisé*. (Right foot front but left shoulder to back corner, i.e. *écarté*.)

1. 2 *brisés dessus*, arms 3rd; *pas de chat*, *pas de bourrée dessous*, arms 5th to 3rd and changing *épaulement*.
2. Repeat on other side.
3. 3 *brisés dessous*, *entrechat quatre*, arms 3rd to *bras bas*.
4. 3 *sissonnes fermées dessus*, *changement*, changing *épaulement* ready to repeat on other side.

Placing – Advanced Centre

4 *Pirouettes* with *poses* taken *en diagonale* [Waltz in 4 bar phrases.]

Commence in 5th *de face* to a corner, head over leading shoulder.

1. *Sissonne ordinaire* into *pas de bourrée dessous*, changing *épaulement* into small 4th *demi-plié* to "spot" corner and *pirouette en dehors*, finishing in a small lunge, i.e. working foot firmly placed on floor behind and body slightly stretched forwards, arms 3rd *arabesque*.
2. Repeat *sissonne*, etc., and finish *pirouette en attitude*.
3. Repeat *sissonne*, etc., finishing *pirouette* in 3rd *arabesque*.
4. *Relevé* in *arabesque*, prepare in 4th for *pirouette en dedans en attitude*. Hold.

Repeat on other side.

5 (*Petit allegro*) [6/8 in 2 bar phrases.]

Commence in 5th *de face*.

1. *Glissade derrière*, *assemblé battu dessus*, *glissade dessous – dessus*.
2. *Glissade devant*, *assemblé battu dessous* (ensure that student uses a good *demi-plié* at beginning and end of *glissade*), *entrechat six*. Repeat on other side.

N.B. Ensure that the student maintains placing and does not get confused with the changing directions.

6 and **7** (*Grand allegro*) [2/4 in 4 bar or 4/4 in 2 bar phrases.]

Commence in 5th *écarté*.

1. *Ballonné écarté* (working leg finishing *retiré devant*), *assemblé porté* closing 5th *devant*; *entrechat trois derrière*, *pas marché en tournant en dehors* into –
2. *Assemblé battu derrière* (making one complete turn in all) 2 *brisés dessous*, *changement* ready to repeat on other side.

36 *Grand ports de bras* (Sharon McGorian)

Placing – Elementary Centre

7 (*Grand allegro*) [6/8 in 2 bar phrases.]

Commence in 3rd or 5th *croisé.*

1. *Soubresaut, échappé fermé* in 4th, *changement* changing *épaulement.*
2. Repeat on other side but finish *de face.*
3. *Glissade derrière, jeté derrière* and repeat on other side.
4. *Coupé, assemblé devant, changement* changing *épaulement*, ready to repeat on other side.

8 (*Grand allegro*) [Grand waltz in 4 bar phrases.]

Commence *pointe tendue* with right foot, *effacé devant.*

4 *balancés* or *pas de valse en tournant*, i.e. step forward right arm to 2nd, circle left foot forwards making a half turn and bending slightly over left side, left arm dropping to *bras bas*, complete turn on right foot; the second *balancé* is almost *en place. Temps levé* into low *arabesque à deux bras, glissade derrière* and repeat *temps levé* into *arabesque* on other foot, ready to repeat.

This should be danced round the studio.

9 *Ports de bras* 'The Waves' [6/8 in 2 bar phrases.]

Commence in 5th *croisé, bras bas* , head lowered, eyes focused on hands.

1. Raise head and arms to 1st. Open arms to 2nd, palms facing front and turn head towards front hand. Straighten head and raise both arms softly to head ·level turning palms down and allowing fingers to press against the air. Lower arms to 2nd, turning palms front.
2. Lower arms to *bras bas* and raise through 1st to open simultaneously into 4th with a *fondu* to *pointe tendue devant.* Bending body and head slightly forwards, circle raised arm downwards into low *arabesque*, i.e. as if bowing over foot. Close 5th *devant* into *assemblé*, ready to repeat on other side.

N.B. The whole must be very flowing and never stop in a pose.

7 (*Grand allegro*) [Strong 3/4 in 2 bar phrases.]

Commence in 5th *croisé*.

1. *Pas de basque élancé en avant* into *assemblé* finishing 5th (arms move from 3rd to *attitude* and *bras bas*), 2 *sissonnes fermées en avant*, arms in 3rd *arabesque*, hold.

2. 3 *retirés posés en arrière* (diagonally backwards), arms 3rd; *posé en avant* into *arabesque à deux bras*, close 5th *derrière*. *Soubresaut*, ready to repeat on other side.

8 (*Grand allegro*) [Mazurka in 2 bar phrases.]

Commence in 5th *de face*.

1. 1 *grande sissonne ouverte à la 2nde, pas de bourrée dessous*, arms from 1st to open 4th and *bras bas*.

2. Repeat on other side.

3. *Grande sissonne ouverte croisé en avant, coupé assemblé dessus*, arms 5th to 1st.

4. Repeat on other side.

5 – 6. Repeat phrases 1 – 2.

7 – 8. 2 runs into *grand jeté en avant*, *posé* into *arabesque* and hold.

8 (*Grand allegro*) *Temps lié* from *sissonnes en tournant en l'air* [Tango and turn on anacrusis.]

Commence in 5th *croisé*.

From 5th *demi-plié, sissonne ordinaire en tournant* into *chassé porté en avant* and *assemblé derrière*. (This means that before landing from what is like a small *tour en l'air*, lift the front leg into low *retiré* and direct it as far forwards as possible on the floor, led by the head and body so that the dancer travels even further forwards on the *assemblé*.

Repeat whole *à la 2nde*, closing 5th *devant*, ready to repeat on other side.

N.B. Arms are very important. They must move from 3rd to 1st and 3rd *arabesque* when travelling forwards and sweep from the *arabesque* to 3rd, 1st and 2nd when moving sideways, before closing *bras bas* and moving swiftly to 3rd as the feet close 5th *devant*, ready for the next *tour*.

9 *Pirouettes en dehors en diagonale* 'Lame Ducks' [2/4.]

Commence *pointe tendue devant*, etc. (see page 41).

Step forwards with the right foot to corner, circle and step on to the left foot *demi-pointe* slightly forwards and making three-quarter turn (i.e. right completes turn). *Coupé* ready to repeat in series.

N.B. Placing is all important. The amount of turn and the arms must be controlled, particularly the circling of the leg forwards, which must be small. It can only be achieved if the dancer steps directly over and stretches upwards onto the supporting leg with torso and head erect. There must be no sinking into the hips as the dancer steps on the *demi-* or full *pointe* with the knee fully stretched and tight.

9 *Pirouettes posées en manège* [2/4.]

Commence *pointe tendue*, etc. and repeat for Ex.9 page 41).

The head and leading foot must anticipate and circle a little further round on each *posé*, by focusing on that point in the imaginary circle at which each particular *pirouette* must finish if the next is to continue the round of the circle. At the beginning of training it is useful to suggest that the dancer travels in a square, i.e. focuses on each corner of the studio in turn. Later it is best to envisage the spacing on a stage, i.e. start at side above stage manager's box, then focus on the conductor or centre of the house, midway up the other side and then centre back stage.

Laws of Balance

PRINCIPLE

'The weight of the body must always be centred over one or both feet and the natural laws of balance be followed at all times in classical dance.'

1. The Natural Law of Opposition

   Always use the opposite arm forwards to leg in front, whether it is working or supporting, particularly when dancing in alignment.

2. The Natural Law of *Epaulement*

   Always bring the same shoulder and arm forwards as foot resting or coming in front whether it is working or supporting. At the same time slightly turn the upper torso and shoulders over that foot when working in *épaulement*.

The aim of this set of classes is to establish Balance whilst maintaining Stance, Turn-out and Placing, particularly in *adage* and *pirouettes*. Students must be encouraged to understand how essential it is to counter-balance their limbs, body and head with each other by strictly controlling their movements at all times. They must follow the two laws set out above and the rules set out below.

RULES

A The head is the heaviest part of the body and it must always move correctly to maintain the central line of balance. It must therefore always lead the movement and anticipate the line to be drawn. (pages 10, 96)

B The arms and legs must never cross the centre line and must be used to counter-balance each other.

C It is better to concentrate on the supporting leg and side, with the weight held fully centred over that foot, than on the height of the raised leg.

D Do not twist the hips in order to achieve turn-out and extension when the working leg is held over 90°.

FOCAL POINTS:

1 The hip line (see page 5).
2 The upper torso (see page 6).
3 Legs (see page 6).
4 Action of feet and legs (see page 7).
5 The head (see page 10).

(see photos 37 a and b, 38, 39, 40, 41, 42, 43, 44 a, b and c)

1 *Pliés* as practice for jumps [Slow 4/4 in 2 bar phrases. Note timing.]

Fokine said, 'You spend twice as long in the air as you do in a *plié* for the preparation.'

Commence in 1st.

1. 2 *demi-pliés* taking 2 beats to descend and 2 to ascend.
2. (1-2-3) Slow full *plié*. (4) Press heels into the floor. (5-6-7-8) Rise straight up through fully stretched legs to *demi-pointes*.

Repeat twice in all, then in 2nd and 5th positions.

N.B. This quick press into and out of the floor by the heels is essential in any type of jump or *relevé*.

2 *Battements tendus* introducing a quickening of tempos [4/4 in 2 bar phrases, note timing.]

Commence in 3rd or 5th.

(1-2-3-4-) *Battement tendu devant*, closing 5th. (1-2) *Battement tendu*, closing 5th. (3-4) 2 *battements tendus*, closing 5th.

Repeat *en croix*.

3 *Battements glissés* using similar timing as **2** above [2/4 in 2 bar phrases.]

Commence in 3rd or 5th.

(1-2) 1 slow *glissé devant* to 20° and close 5th. (3-4) 2 quick *glissés*, closing 5th.

Repeat *en croix*. Then repeat, rising into slow *glissé* and closing 5th *demi-plié* on second quick one.

Laws of Balance – Intermediate *Barre*

1 *Pliés* [Slow waltz in 4 bar or 6/8 in 2 bar phrases.]

Commence in 5th.

1. Rise on *demi-pointes*, opening leg *à la 2nde*, close 1st and drop heels, *demi-plié*.
2 – 3. 2 full *pliés* in 1st.
4. Rise with *ports de bras* as for Intermediate Stance (see page 27). Repeat rise, opening into 2nd, then into 4th opposite 5th and 5th.

N.B. It is essential to control the opening of the leg. The student must follow the toe down into the open positions and hold the weight away from the legs. Even if the 2nd position seems too small, the full *plié* should be attempted as the stretch away and height from the body must be exact. Moreover, before the *plié* begins, the placing of the weight centrally over both feet is vital to stability and turn-out.

2 *Battements tendus* [Steady 2/4 in 2 bar phrases or 4/4.]

1. *Tendu devant* and *à la 2nde*, closing 5th *devant-derrière*.
2. *Pointe tendue derrière*, pass through 1st to *pointe tendue devant* and return to *pointe tendue derrière* and close 5th. Repeat in reverse. Then repeat whole.

N.B. The head and upper torso must move very slightly, i.e. when moving *devant*, stretch very slightly upwards and back; when *à la 2nde*, straighten and turn head towards working arm; when moving *derrière*, bend slightly forwards, head inclined over supporting side, and during the passing through 1st use a very slight movement back and front. The arm is opened from 1st to 2nd and held still until the feet close, then moved to *bras bas*.

3 *Battements glissés* with *demi-ronds* [Steady 2/4 in 2 bar phrases.]

Commence in 5th

(1-2) *Relevé* with *glissé devant* to 20°, close 5th lowering heels. (and-3, and-4) 2 *glissés* dropping to *pointe piquée*, the second circling *à la 2nde*, and closing 5th *demi-plié*.

Repeat from *à la 2nde* to *derrière* and then in reverse. Repeat whole.

N.B. Open the arm through 1st to 2nd and hold till closing in *demi-plié*. In *pointe piquée* the tips of the toes lightly touch the floor as the leg descends and rebounds for a moment before circling. Keep the hips very still.

Laws of Balance – Advanced *Barre*

1 *Pliés*

Repeat as for Intermediate *pliés*, opening arms from 1st to 5th and 2nd during preparation for *plié*.

2 *Battements tendus* with quarter turns [2/4 in 4 bar phrases.]

Commence in 5th.

1. 1 *tendu devant* and a second closing 5th *demi-plié* and making a quarter turn towards the *barre*, closing 5th *devant*.
2. Repeat above, moving *à la 2nde* and closing 5th *demi-plié derrière* before the quarter turn.
3 – 4. 4 *tendus en croix*, each closing in *demi-plié*. Repeat on other side and then in reverse.

3 *Battements glissés* with *relevés* into quarter turns [3/4 or tarantella in 2 bar phrases.]

Commence in 5th.

2 *glissés devant*, the second closing in 5th *demi-plié*, *relevé* and quarter turn to *barre*, holding *glissé à la 2nde* before closing. Then continue as **2** above, using 2 sets of *glissés en croix* during the last phrase.

37 *Attitudes* (Phillip Broomhead) –
note the line centred over the
balancing board: *a* Mercury;
b classical *attitude*

4 *Ronds de jambe à terre* as preparation for *pas de basque* [3/4 in 4 bar phrases.]

Commence in 1st, 3rd or 5th.

1. 3 *ronds à terre en dehors* circling *devant* – *à la 2nde* – 1st only and one full *rond* closing 1st.
2. Repeat *en dedans* circling *à la 2nde* – *derrière* – 1st and 1 full *rond*.

Repeat *en dedans*.

N.B. Placing must be exact with heel firmly pressed down in 1st and no twisting of the hips.

5 *Grands battements* for strengthening the 'muscular corset' [Slow waltz in 2 bar phrases.]

Commence in 3rd or 5th.

1. Slowly lift leg *devant* to 90°, i.e. *battement relevé*, hold and close.
2. 2 *battements devant* with accent up on first beat, held for a second and closing on third beat.

Repeat *en croix* and use simple *ports de bras* for slow *battement*.

6 *Petits battements* as an introduction to half-turns [2/4 in 2 bar phrases.]

Commence *sur le cou de pied*.

2 *petits battements* beating *derrière* – *devant* twice, close 5th *devant demi-plié* and rise into a half turn *en dehors*, close 5th *derrière*. Working arm rises to 1st and other arm leaves the *barre* before closing to it. New supporting arm rests on *barre* just as the feet close, NOT BEFORE.

Repeat on other side.

Later repeat with *retiré passé* on half turn and return to same side with half turn *en dedans*. In this case the half turn will be on the same supporting leg. It is therefore very important to ensure the correct focusing of the eyes.

Laws of Balance – Intermediate *Barre*

4 *Ronds de jambe* with *développés* [3/4 in 2 bar phrases or 6/8.]

Commence in 5th.

    1. *Développé devant* at 45°, drop to *pointe tendue* and slow *rond en dehors*, closing 5th *derrière*.

    2. Repeat in reverse.

    Use arms opening from 1st to 5th and 2nd with each *développé devant* and from 1st to *arabesque* with *développé derrière*.

    3 – 4. 4 *ronds en dehors*, closing 5th *derrière*, then 4 *ronds en dedans*. Repeat whole rising into each *développé*.

N.B. Ensure that the dancer closes the feet tightly together after the slow *rond*, in order to feel the impetus needed to lift the leg later when jumping.

5 *Grands battements* with rises to strengthen the 'muscular corset' [4/4 in 2 bar phrases.]

Commence in 5th.

    (1) Rise on *demi-pointes*, arms to 5th. (2) *Battement devant*. (3) Close 5th *demi-pointes*. (4) Lower heels. (1-2-3-4) 2 *grands battements devant*, lowering arm to 2nd.

Repeat *en croix*. Raise arm to 5th when *à la 2nde* and from 5th to *arabesque* when working *derrière*.

N.B. As in **4** above, ensure that the dancer closes the feet tightly together on *demi-pointes* before lowering heels and ensure that the weight is held momentarily over both feet before the two *battements*. Use the arms very clearly and co-ordinate the arm movement absolutely with the leg movement.

6 *Petits ronds de jambe en l'air* [Mazurka in 2 bar phrases.]

Commence in 5th.

    Chassé en avant, but do not transfer weight, take weight on back foot stretching both knees and into *battement glissé devant* circling to *à la 2nde* at 45° (later 90°). 2 *petits ronds de jambe en l'air en dehors*, close 5th *derrière*.

Repeat moving *derrière* and *en dedans*.

N.B. It is essential to press into and out of the floor during the *chassé* and *glissé* to gain impetus for the *ronds*. This is useful practice for later *petits ronds sautés*. Ensure that the hips do not twist and that the weight is properly centred over the supporting leg. Also practise rising *sur les pointes*.

Laws of Balance – Advanced *Barre*

4 *Ronds de jambe* with *grands ronds jetés*

    Repeat as for Turn-out (page 45) but pass through 1st into *attitude devant en fondu* then throw leg round in a circling line to finish momentarily in *arabesque*.

    Repeat 3 times in all and hold last *arabesque en fondu*, arm in open 5th, eyes glancing at upraised hand. Close. Repeat in reverse.

N.B. It is essential that the supporting leg stretches as the working leg reaches its height *à la 2nde* and the arm opens as it reaches *arabesque*.

5 *Grands battements* [Mazurka in 2 bar phrases, accent must be up on the 1st beat, hold position on 2nd beat and close on 3rd.]

Commence in 5th.

    1. 2 *battements devant* at 90° and a third which passes through *retiré* to *arabesque*. Hold. Close 5th.

    2. Repeat in reverse.

    3 – 4. Repeat twice *à la 2nde*, bringing leg back to *retiré* after third *battement*, then closing 5th *derrière*. On repeat, close *devant*.

Repeat *sur les demi-pointes*.

6 *Battements fondus en croix* [6/8 in 2 bar phrases.]

Commence in 5th.

    1. *Fondu* into *retiré devant* and *relevé développé devant* at 45°.

    2. Repeat *à la 2nde*.

    3 – 4. Repeat *derrière* and *à la 2nde*.

Repeat raising to 90°. Hold last *arabesque*, swing leg through 1st *sur demi-pointes*, close 5th and *détourné*, ready to repeat on other side.

N.B. Ensure that the heel of the supporting leg is flat on the floor before the knee bends in *fondu*, and that the knee straightens before the *relevé*. This is essential if the movement of unfolding the leg is to be stable and continuous.

7 *Battements frappés* with rises and hold [Tango in 2 bar phrases.]
2 *frappés devant* returning to *sur le cou de pied*. *Relevé*, raising working leg to *retiré* and hold.

Repeat *en croix*.

38   *Attitude,* from *Napoli* (Karen Paisey)

39   *Développé devant en fondu,* from *La Bayadère* (Fiona Chadwick)

8 *Adage* Introducing *demi-grands ronds de jambe* [6/8, sarabande or minuet in 2 bar phrases.]
Commence in 1st, 3rd or 5th.

1. *Développé devant* at 90°, circle *à la 2nde* and close 5th *derrière*, arm moving from *bras bas* to 1st and 2nd to *bras bas*.
2. Repeat, circling from *à la 2nde – derrière*. Use conventional *ports de bras*, raising arm to 1st simultaneously with *retiré* and opening to 2nd with *développé*.

Repeat, moving *en dedans*. Here it is valuable to raise the arm from 2nd to 5th before stretching to *arabesque* and from 2nd to 5th when moving from *à la 2nde* to *devant*. This helps to keep the weight centred and away from the hips.

9 Preparation for *pointes, posés* and *relevés* [3/4 in 2 bar phrases.]
Commence in 5th, facing and with both hands on *barre*.

1. Step on *pointe derrière* as close as possible to the supporting leg with *retiré*, i.e. *posé*, hold, *coupé*. Repeat *posé*, closing 5th *devant*.
2. *Relevé retiré devant*, hold, lower heel. *Relevé retiré passé* and close 5th *derrière*, *demi-plié*. Ready to repeat with other foot.

Repeat 4 times in all.

Laws of Balance – Intermediate *Barre*

7 *Petits battements* into *petits posés* [Waltz in 4 bar phrases.]

Commence *sur le cou de pied*.

1. *Petits battements sur le cou de pied de face, demi-bras* (please keep time, beating *derrière – devant* as accurately as possible). *Fondu* and *développé effacé* to *pointe tendue devant*, slightly bending over leg with arm in 1st.
2. Repeat above and move into *à la 2nde*, arm to 2nd, body straight.
3. Repeat to *effacé derrière*, arm to 2nd *arabesque*.
4. Rise with *rond de jambe en dedans* at 45°, close 5th *demi-pointes* and *détourné*, ready to repeat on other side. Repeat in reverse, turning *effacé*. Then repeat whole, turning *croisé* with *détourné en dehors*.

8 *Adage* [Grand waltz or minuet in 2 bar phrases or slow 6/8.]

Commence in 5th.

1. Simultaneously *fondu* and *pointe tendue devant* with right foot, raise leg *devant* to 90°, arm to 5th as supporting leg stretches.
2. *Grand rond en dehors*, arm falling from 5th to 1st and 2nd.
3. *Fouetté relevé* into *arabesque penchée*, arm to 5th.
4. Recover and *retiré*, raise arm to 5th and *ports de bras* backwards, close 5th and repeat on other side.

This should also be repeated in reverse at a later stage.

9 Preparation for *pirouettes sur les pointes* [Steady 2/4 or 3/4.]

Commence in 5th.

Relevé retiré passé derrière into small 4th *demi-plié*, arms 1st. *Relevé* into *pirouette en dehors sur la pointe*, finishing 5th *demi-plié*.

Repeat at least 4 times using same foot.

N.B. Both heels must be firmly pressed into the floor before the *relevé* into the *pirouette* and the *retiré* should be held as the supporting leg sinks into *fondu* at the end of the *pirouette*. Only then should the working leg descend into 5th.

Laws of Balance – Advanced *Barre*

7 *Petits battements* with *fondus* and *relevés* [Gallop.]

Commence *sur le cou de pied*.

With supporting leg straight, 8 *petits battements*; repeat series of *battements* whilst sinking *en fondu*, gradually bending the working foot upwards at ankle; slowly rise, still beating and gradually straightening the supporting knee, and continue upwards on to *demi-pointe*, gradually pointing working foot until it is fully stretched, toe just above the other ankle bone.

N.B. The beat must be right across the ankle throughout, the movement must be continuous and the working foot gradually respond to the changes in height from the floor. The ideal is to find the tips only leave the floor as the fully stretched supporting leg begins to rise *sur les demi-pointes*.

8 *Adage* [Slow waltz in 2 bar phrases.]

Commence in 5th.

1. *Grand rond de jambe en dehors* into 2 slow *fouettés relevés*, arm moving from *arabesque* to 5th and 2nd, and 1st, 5th to *arabesque*.
2. Drop to *pointe tendue derrière* and *ports de bras devant* and *derrière*.
3. Raise to 90° and *grand rond de jambe en dedans*.
4. *Relevé* and rotate to *arabesque*.

9 Practice for *grands fouettés* and rotation *sur les pointes*

Repeat as for Exercise 9 page 47 but take very slowly and rise to full *pointe* each time the leg swings front or back and hold *sur la pointe* during rotation to new pose.

Laws of Balance – Elementary Centre

1 (*Petit adage*) [4/4 in 2 bar phrases.]

Commence in 5th *croisé*.

1. Full *plié*. *Battement tendu devant*, closing 3rd or 5th. 2 *glissés devant*.
2. Repeat *tendu* and *glissés derrière*. **Tendu à la 2nde** circling *derrière* into small 4th for *pirouette en dehors*, closing 5th *derrière*, ready to repeat on other side.

2 (*Petit adage*) [Waltz in 4 bar phrases.]

Commence in 5th *croisé*.

1. 2 *ronds à terre en dehors*, changing *épaulement* to *de face* and finishing *pointe tendue devant*. Pass through 1st to *pointe tendue derrière* and again to *pointe tendue devant*.
2. Repeat, changing *épaulement* to next corner and close 5th *devant*.
3. 4 *ronds en dedans*.
4. A fifth *rond* finishing *pointe tendue derrière*, dropping into small 4th for *pirouette en dehors*, ready to repeat on other side.

3 (*Grand adage*) *ADAGE* [Minuet or slow waltz in 4 bar phrases.]

1. *Développé écarté devant*, circle *devant* raising arms to 5th and *tombé* into *ports de bras*, stretch and close 5th *derrière*.
2. Using back foot, *développé écarté derrière*, circle to 3rd *arabesque, fondu* stretching to *pointe tendue derrière* and *pas de bourrée dessous*, ready to repeat on other side.

40 *Arabesque penchée,* from *La Bayadère* (Bryony Brind)

Laws of Balance – Intermediate Centre

1 (*Petit adage*) [4/4 in 4 bar phrases.]

Commence in 5th *croisé*.

Full *plié*. *Battements tendus devant, à la 2nde* and *derrière* – do not close – then pass through 1st to *pointe tendue devant, derrière* (see **2** page 69). Drop into small 4th *derrière* for *pirouette en dehors*, finishing 5th *devant*. Immediately move into another *pirouette en dehors*, finishing 5th *devant*, ready to repeat on other side. (Pick up front foot in *pirouettes*.)

2 (*Petit adage*) [Waltz in 4 bar phrases.]

Commence in 5th *croisé*.

1. *Glissade en avant, ronds à terre en dehors*, closing 5th *derrière*. Repeat in reverse.
2. *Glissade derrière* into *relevé* with *glissé* to 45° and 2 *petits ronds de jambe en l'air*. Repeat on other side.
3. 4 *ronds en dehors* to change *épaulement* to next corner.
4. A fifth *rond* to *pointe tendue derrière, relevé* into *attitude* and hold. (Or *pirouette en dedans en attitude*.) Close 5th *derrière*, ready to repeat on other side.

3 (*Grand adage*) ADAGE [Sarabande in 2 bar phrases.]

Commence in 5th *croisé*.

1. *Glissade écarté derrière, développé écarté devant* and circle to 2nd *arabesque*.
2. Rotate to *effacé devant* at 90°, pass through 1st to 3rd *arabesque* and raise to *attitude*.
3 – 4. *Pas de bourrée en tournant en dehors*, finishing 5th; *grand rond de jambe en dehors, fondu* with stretch into *pas de bourrée dessous*, passing foot *devant* into 4th *croisé; relevé* into *retiré passé*, closing 5th *devant*, ready to repeat on other side.

Laws of Balance – Advanced Centre

1 (*Petit adage*) [4/4 in 2 bar phrases.]

Commence in 5th *croisé*.

1. *Relevé* into one slow *battement tendu devant* (i.e. rise and stretch working leg forwards without allowing toe to leave floor), close 5th then lower heels; 2 quick *glissés* and low *développé* into *pas marché en avant sur les demi-pointes*.
2. Repeat moving *en arrière*.
3. *Pointe tendue devant* to 4th and full *plié* and recover to *demi-plié*, then *pirouette en dehors*, finishing 5th *devant* on opposite side.
4. *Relevé* and *glissé devant* into small 4th and *pirouette en dehors*, finishing 5th *devant* and repeat, i.e. pick up front foot.

N.B. The arms must be in complete control during the *pirouettes*. There should be no extra *demi-plié* at the beginning of the second *pirouette*, so the position must be very accurate and the finish in *demi-plié* always very firmly placed.

2 (*Petit adage*) [Waltz in 8 bar phrases.]

Commence in 5th *croisé*.

1. 4 *ronds en dehors*, the fourth passing through 1st to *attitude devant en fondu*, throw leg *à la 2nde* and circle downwards to *pointe tendue derrière* as preparation for *pirouette en dedans*, finishing 5th *devant*.
2. Repeat 4 *ronds en dedans*, changing *épaulement* and finishing *attitude effacée*. Throw *à la 2nde* and circle to *pointe tendue devant*, move into small 4th *demi-plié* and *pirouette en dehors*, finishing 5th *derrière*, ready to repeat on other side.

N.B. Carefully note the use of the arm at the *barre* during the throw to the side. When exercising in the centre, use the same *ports de bras*, but keep under very strict control.

3 (*Grand adage*) ADAGE [Minuet in 4 bar phrases.]

Commence in 5th *croisé*.

1. *Relevé à deux bras, pas marché en avant* (i.e. use back foot) into 1st *arabesque*, rotate to 4th *devant* at 90°, pass through 1st to 3rd *arabesque*.
2. *Voyagé* towards raised leg, pass through 1st into *pas marché en arrière* and lift to *attitude*.
3. *Voyagé* towards supporting leg, pass through 1st to *devant* at 90°.
4. *Tombé*, finishing *pointe tendue derrière* and *ports de bras*.

N.B. Throughout ensure that the supporting leg works correctly during the *voyagés*, i.e. the turn should be performed on quarter point so that the heel is slightly lifted from the floor, weight directly centred over the supporting leg. On no account misplace the relationship between the body in alignment with that leg.

41   Classical *arabesque* (Julie Rose)

4 Practice for *pirouettes en dedans* with or without *fouetté* [Waltz in 4 bar phrases.]

Version 1 with *fouetté*. Commence in 5th *de face*.

Pointe tendue derrière, arms 1st to 2nd, *fondu* and drop back heel without moving body so that weight is still centred over front foot, arms 3rd. *Glissé derrière* and immediately circle *à la 2nde* into *relevé retiré*, bringing arms to 1st. Hold and close 5th *devant*. Repeat 4 times in all.

Version 2 without *fouetté*. Commence in 5th *de face*.

Pointe tendue derrière, *fondu* and drop heel as above, simultaneously *relevé retiré*, hold and close 5th *devant*.

N.B. *Pirouettes en dedans* should be practised with and without the *fouetté* preparation. In both much care is needed to ensure that the body is erect, weight centred over the supporting leg *en fondu*. The next important feature is to ensure that the working leg moves and is exactly timed. When using the *fouetté* preparation, the leg must rise and circle precisely from back to side before it is whipped into *retiré* with the *relevé* into the turn. When turning without the *fouetté*, the working leg must be drawn straight into the *retiré* with the *relevé* into the turn. The toe should reach mid-calf at the side of the supporting leg before coming front, or back – whichever is required for the next movement (see page 13).

5 (*Petit allegro*) [2/4 in 2 bar phrases.]

Commence in 5th *de face*.

1.   2 *petits jetés derrière, coupé, assemblé dessous*.
2.   3 *glissades dessous – dessus – dessous, changement battu*, ready to repeat on other side.

N.B. It is essential to ensure that the head is always over the foot coming or resting in front.

42   Sword thrust into *arabesque*, from MacMillan's *Romeo and Juliet* (Michael Batchelor)

Laws of Balance – Intermediate Centre

4 *Pirouettes* with *posés* [Tango in 2 bar phrases.]

Commence in 5th *effacé*.

1. *Posé* into *attitude croisée devant*, drop into small 4th *demi-plié* and *pirouette en dehors*, finishing *pointe tendue derrière*.
2. *Posé en arrière* into low *arabesque* (working leg must pass through 1st), drop into 4th and *pirouette en dedans*, arms 5th (without *fouetté*) and finishing 5th *devant*.
3. *Glissade derrière* and *posé* into *attitude croisée*, repeat on other side.
4. Close 5th *derrière*, *échappé* into 4th and *pirouette en dehors*, arms 5th and closing 5th *derrière*, ready to repeat on other side.

5 (*Petit allegro*) [2/4, dance very evenly to each beat.]

Commence in 5th *de face*.

2 *petits jetés battus dessus*, *coupé dessous*, 2 *brisés dessus*, *pas de bourrée piqué dessous*, *entrechat quatre* and hold ready to repeat on other side.

Laws of Balance – Advanced Centre

4 *Pirouettes* [2/4 in 2 bar phrases.]

Commence in 5th *croisé*.

1. (and-1, and-2, and-3,4) *Relevé* and hold *sur demi-pointe*, 2 *retirés passés. Glissé devant* into small 4th *demi-plié. Pirouette en dehors*, finishing 5th *devant* on other side.
2. Repeat, using other foot but *pirouette en dedans*, finishing 5th *devant* on other side.
3. *Relevé glissé devant* into small 4th *demi-plié* and *pirouette en dehors*, finishing *pointe tendue à la 2nde*.
4. *Pas de bourrée dessous* into 4th *demi-plié* and *pirouette en dedans*, finishing 5th *devant*, ready to repeat on other side.

5 (*Petit allegro*) *Temps lié* with slow *pirouettes* and *ports de bras* [Very slow waltz in 4 bar phrases and commence on anacrusis.]

1. *Pirouette en dehors* (pick up front foot), *chassé en avant* (i.e. the raised foot does not close 5th but slides forwards) as far as possible, close 5th *derrière* with arms to 4th. *Ports de bras* forwards from the waist only, arms moving from 3rd to 3rd when bending straight forwards and rising to open 4th and 3rd, ready to repeat.
2. *Pirouette en dehors*, *chassé à la 2nde*, close 5th *devant*, arms to open 4th and *ports de bras* bending and circling sideways and slightly backwards to other side, arms moving from 4th to 4th, 2nd and 3rd ready to repeat all with other foot.

N.B. The arms do not sink to *bras bas* throughout. The change at the front or back is made directly from side to side, i.e. as the body bends forwards the one arm falls to 3rd, both arms then change before the body straightens. The same happens as the body bends backwards.

6 (*Petit allegro*) [2/4 in 2 bar phrases.]

Commence in 5th *de face*.

1. *Glissade, petit jeté derrière, temps levé* in *attitude, assemblé derrière*.
2. Repeat on other side.
3. Turn into *coupé ballotté effacé devant* and *derrière, pas marché*, turning to back corner, and *assemblé derrière* (i.e. back to audience).
4. 2 *petits jetés derrière* and *petit assemblé devant*, continuing to turn and finishing *de face*, ready to repeat on other side.

7 (*Grand allegro*) [Strong 3/4 in 2 bar phrases.]

Commence in 5th *croisé*.

1. *Pas de basque sauté en avant* changing *épaulement*, 2 *changements*, changing *épaulement* very slightly on each, *entrechat quatre*.
2. Repeat on other side.
3. 2 *pas de basque sautés en arrière*.
4. 3 *glissades dessous – dessus – dessous, entrechat quatre*, hold and be ready to repeat on other side.

N.B. It is essential to remember changes in *épaulement* during the *pas de basque, changements* and *entrechat quatre* in contrast to the *glissades* which should be *de face*. Make a distinction between the *pas de basque* which should be slightly *élancé* and the *glissades* which must be glided and smooth. Use conventional arms and head.

8 (*Grand allegro*) [2/4 in 2 bar phrases.]

Commence in 5th *de face*.

1. *Jeté porté à la 2nde* (use front foot so that working foot finishes *retiré devant*), *temps levé* in *attitude devant*, turn into *jeté croisé avant* in *attitude* and *temps levé* in *attitude*.
2. 2 *petits jetés derrière*, continuing to turn and coming *de face* with legs in low *attitude derrière*. *Assemblé* with *bras bas*, ready to repeat on other side.

43   Odette's *arabesque*, from *Swan Lake* (Bryony Brind)

Laws of Balance – Intermediate Centre

6 (*Petit allegro*) *Fouettés relevés* [5/4, note timing.]

Commence *pointe tendue devant*, facing side of studio.

(1) *Posé devant*, raising leg to 90° *devant*. (2) Rotate to *arabesque*. (3) *Fondu*. (4) Pass through 1st into *chassé en avant*. (5) Transfer weight and stretch other foot to *pointe tendue devant*, ready to repeat on other side.

Once mastered this should also be attempted by performing the first *fouetté* and holding the *arabesque fondue* for the third and fourth beats. Close 5th *derrière* and then stretch the other foot *pointe tendue devant* to repeat on other side.

7 (*Grand allegro*) [Waltz in 4 bar phrases.]

Commence in 5th *de face*.

1. *Sissonne ouverte à la 2nde, pas de bourrée dessous*. Repeat on other side.
2. *Sissonne ouverte croisé en avant, coupé, assemblé en avant*. Repeat on other side.
3. *Temps levé* into *fouetté sauté*, pass through 1st and repeat on other side.
4. 3 runs into *grand jeté en avant* and *relevé* into *arabesque*. Hold.

8 (*Grand allegro*) *Temps lié* with *sissonnes fermées* and *ouvertes* [Tarantella in 2 bar phrases.]

Commence in 5th *croisé*.

1. *Sissonne ouverte en avant, assemblé derrière*, 2 *sissonnes fermées en avant*. Hold in 5th.
2. *Sissonne ouverte à la 2nde*. Hold pose. 2 *sissonnes fermées à la 2nde*, closing *dessous – dessus*, ready to repeat on other side.

This should also be practised in reverse.

Laws of Balance – Advanced Centre

6 (*Petit allegro*) [2/4 and dance to each beat.]

Commence in 5th *croisé*.

Brisés volés en avant and *en arrière, brisé dessous, pas de chat.*

Repeat 4 times in all, and then with other foot.

N.B. The arms must be kept very simple and move from 1st to 2nd and 3rd. Hips and shoulders must be held parallel and as far as possible facing the same plane, as the purpose of the exercise is the correct placing of the beats. Therefore, a slight use of *épaulement* should be made and the body kept flexible.

7 (*Grand allegro*) *Fouettés relevés sur les pointes* [6/8.]

Commence *pointe tendue croisé devant*.

Posé devant at 90°, *fouetté* into 1st *arabesque* (hold supporting leg *sur pointe*), *pas de bourrée en avant* and *en arrière* and *en tournant en dedans*. On third step, *posé* and *fouetté* as before, *tombé* and repeat *fouetté*, ready to repeat whole on same side once more.

8 (*Grand allegro*) *Tours en l'air* (boys) and *pirouettes fouettées en tournant* (girls)

Boys commence in 5th *de face*. [Gallop or 2/4.]

Soubresaut en place finishing 5th *demi-plié*, arms 3rd, and immediately into *tour l'air*, changing feet in the air. Finish *demi-plié*, ready to repeat *soubresaut* and *tour* on the other side.

Once this has been mastered, greater impetus is gained by the following:

Chassé – coupé assemblé en avant, relevé (or *soubresaut*) into good *demi-plié* and then double *tour en l'air*.

Continued page 81.

44 Aurora rises to her Prince, from *The Sleeping Beauty* (Fiona Chadwick and Nicholas Dixon): *a* Prepare by centring the weight over the supporting foot;

b Gradually stretch upwards, still centred;

c The triumphant *attitude*.

9 *Ports de bras* 'The *arabesques*' [Minuet or waltz in 8 bar phrases. Bar number is given.]

Commence in 5th *effacé bras bas*, head turned over front (left) shoulder.

1. *Chassé en avant* to *pointe tendue derrière*, opening arms through 1st to 1st *arabesque* and stretching body and head upwards, eyes focused on front hand.
2. Bring arms to 2nd, palms facing floor and head slightly lowered as weight is transferred over two feet.
3. Lower arms, turning and focusing eyes on left hand.
4. Transfer weight to *pointe tendue derrière* (i.e. move forwards) through soft *demi-plié*, circling left arm forwards, right arm backwards and stretching upper torso and head into 2nd *arabesque*.
5. Pass left foot through 1st into *chassé en avant* and *pointe tendue derrière* (i.e. right foot), arms passing through 1st and 2nd with palms down and head turning towards left hand.
6. Circle right arm forwards and slightly upwards, left downwards, stretching body and head outwards into 3rd *arabesque*.
7. Keeping palms down, circle both arms and twist body round and backwards into 4th *arabesque* (i.e. Russian school, the body is turned away from the audience, but the head is turned over the front shoulder).
8. Close 5th *derrière*, lowering arms and head. There should be a slight pause before repeating on the other side.

N.B. It is absolutely essential that the hips and shoulders face the same plane during the 1st, 2nd and 3rd *arabesques* so that the turn of the body and head in 4th *arabesque* is both SEEN and FELT to be different.

Continued from page 79.

Girls commence in two ways. [Gallop.]

Version 1

Pas de bourrée en tournant en dedans (on anacrusis) directly into *fondu*, the working leg stretching *devant* to 45° or higher. Immediately *relevé*, whipping raised leg from side to *retiré* and into the turn. Repeat *fondu* and whip into *relevé – retiré* at least 8 times. Repeat on other side.

Version 2

From small 4th *demi-plié, pirouette en dehors*, finishing as above in *fondu*, working leg stretched *devant*. Then continue to turn at least 8 times, sinking and rising from *fondu* to *relevé* as the working leg whips in and out.

N.B. These *pirouettes* can also be performed with the working leg moving from *à la 2nde* into *retiré* without any circling of the working leg – as in the Russian school.

9 *Pirouettes en diagonale en dehors* and *en dedans* [2/4.]

Commence *pointe tendue devant*, etc. (see pages 41 and 67).

There are two ways to perform these *pirouettes*:

Version 1

Having completed one *pirouette posée en dedans* (on right foot), *coupé* on to left and step on right simultaneously circling left forwards and step on *demi-* or full *pointe* making one turn *en dehors*, finishing *en fondu*, ready to repeat *pirouette en dedans* and thus continue in series.

Version 2

Having mastered the above the turns must now be practised *sur les pointes*, i.e. *posé* into *pirouette en dedans, fondu* and immediately circle other leg forwards and step on *pointe* for *pirouette en dehors*, stepping directly *sur la pointe* for the next *pirouette en dedans*.

Whichever way the *pirouette* turns, the size of the step taken must be directly controlled and never larger than a small 4th.

9 *Grands jetés en avant en tournant en manège* [Steady 2/4.]

Commence in 5th *écarté*, arms 3rd.

Chassé en avant en tournant, closing 5th *derrière* and into *grand jeté en avant*. Bring raised leg into 5th *derrière* making another turn, ready to repeat *grand jeté* – and continue in series.

N.B. The first *chassé* must be well into the floor and downwards to give impetus to the *grand jeté*. It is best to suggest that the back foot always remains behind the leading foot, particularly during the turn immediately after the *jeté*. Arms must be carefully placed from 3rd to 1st and *arabesque* until the *jeté* is mastered. Never allow the back arm in *arabesque* to go far behind the shoulder because the dancer must face forwards during the *jeté* and it must be exactly to the front. Later this movement should be practised *en attitude*.

Transfer of Weight

PRINCIPLE

'Weight must always be transferred from one foot to the other through the centre line of balance.'

These three classes attempt to teach the many ways of transferring weight from one position or step to another whilst maintaining the principles of Stance, Turn-out, Placing and Balance and controlling the movements of the whole body to create a line of dance. This is done by utilising the various ways of stepping, gliding, jumping or darting to fill each individual's square with movements of breadth, width, height and depth. Only by so doing will the varying qualities of classical dance be fully demonstrated even at an Elementary stage.

RULES:

A The dancer must always step, dart, glide or jump exactly into the direction indicated by the head and the outstretched leg and toe, taking the weight over, to and through the central line to the desired point of balance on the now supporting leg. This is of vital importance when landing from any jump or *tombé*, or moving into a *posé* or *relevé sur les pointes*.

B When the movement is forwards the head usually turns towards the foot coming in front, when backwards it usually inclines towards the supporting leg.

C In all conventional *ports de bras* the arms should pass through 1st at the moment of transfer as they move from one position to another. This is particularly important in the early stages of training and vital when the transfer of weight from one foot to the other *à terre* is first practised.

FOCAL POINTS

1 Transfer of weight. (page 10).
2 Height and extension (page 12).
3 Timing movement physically (page 13).

(see photos 45, 46a and b, 47, 48, 49a, b and c)

1 *Pliés*
Repeat as for Laws of Balance (page 68).

2 *Battements tendus* to introduce spacing of *pas marchés* [4/4.]
Commence in 1st, 3rd or 5th.

    Pointe tendue devant, drop heel, transfer to *pointe tendue derrière*, drop heel; transfer to *pointe tendue devant*, drop heel, transfer again and close 5th.

Repeat *derrière* and *à la 2nde* away and towards the *barre*. Repeat again transferring weight through *demi-plié*.

N.B. Once the toe is fully pointed it should not move, the heel merely sinking to the floor. It is essential that the body is held directly upwards from the legs, that the transfer is exact and that there is no over-turning of the working leg when moving behind. Do not bend knees during transfers during first series.

3 *Battements glissés* as practice for landing from jumps [2/4 in 2 bar phrases.]
Commence in 3rd or 5th.

    1. *Glissé devant* to 20°, hold, drop to 4th *en fondu* transferring weight, and lift to 20° *derrière* and close 3rd or 5th.
    2. 4 *glissés derrière*.

Repeat in reverse and twice *à la 2nde* away and towards the *barre*. Repeat whole.

N.B. Each time the dancer transfers weight the supporting leg must sink *en fondu* and it is vital that the leg follows the pointed toe down. It is sometimes useful to dance this to 3/4 as this gives children a chance to hold the *fondu*.

Transfer of Weight – Intermediate *Barre*

1 *Pliés* [4/4.]

Commence in 1st.

Taking 2 bars for each *plié*, perform 2 *pliés* in 1st, 2nd, 4th opposite 5th and 5th, bending the body slightly forwards from the waist only. Arms in 4th, when in 1st; sideways when in 2nd; backwards when in 4th; but keep erect in 5th.

N.B. Only by keeping the spine mobile will the dancer be able to transfer weight correctly and these slight bends in one direction or the other can help them understand that the upper body can help to sustain balance if it responds to the line of the movement.

2 *Battements tendus* [6/8 in 2 bar phrases.]

Commence in 5th.

1. 2 *tendus devant*, the second closing 5th *demi-plié*.
2. Stretch to *pointe tendue devant*, drop heel, transferring weight and stretching up now supporting leg stretch other to *pointe tendue derrière*, close 5th *derrière*.

Repeat moving *derrière* and *à la 2nde* away and towards the *barre*. Repeat in reverse.

N.B. It is essential that the pointed toe indicates exactly where the whole foot will rest as the new supporting leg is stretched (see note pages 10, 12).

3 *Battements glissés* [Steady and strong 3/4, dance to each beat.]

Commence in 5th.

1. Simultaneously *fondu* and *glissé devant* at 20°, hold and transfer, closing 5th *demi-plié* and stretching knees.
2. 3 *glissés derrière*.

Repeat, moving *derrière* and *à la 2nde* away and towards the *barre*.

N.B. The student should be able to hold the second beat *en fondu* and then transfer, closing and straightening the knee on the third beat.

Transfer of Weight – Advanced *Barre*

1 *Pliés*

Repeat as for Turn-out (page 43).

2 *Battements tendus* [5/4 in 2 bar phrases, please note timing.]

(1) *Pointe tendue devant*. (2) Drop heel. (3) Re-point toe. (4) Circle *à la 2nde*. (5) Drop heel.

(1) *Tendue à la 2nde* (i.e. foot nearest *barre*). (2) Drop heel. (3) *Tendue à la 2nde* using other foot. (4) Close 5th *devant*. (5) Quick *battement tendu à la 2nde*, closing 5th *derrière*.

Repeat in reverse. Then repeat dropping into *demi-pliés* in all the open positions.

3 *Battements glissés* as practice for landing from jumps [Strong 3/4 in 2 bar phrases or 6/8 with 6 strong beats.]

Commence in 5th

1. Simultaneously *fondu* and *glissé devant* at 20°, transfer weight *en fondu*, hold.
2. Transfer weight *derrière en fondu* and again forwards, then close 5th *derrière*.

Repeat *derrière* and *à la 2nde* away and towards the *barre*.

N.B. It is useful to give a slight spring on each transfer, but ensure that the hips do not rock or twist. Anticipate with the head the direction to be travelled.

45 Florestan's *grand jeté en avant*, from *The Sleeping Beauty* (Phillip Broomhead)

4 *Ronds de jambe* with transfers *à terre* [Slow waltz in 2 bar phrases or 6/8.]

Commence in 1st, 3rd or 5th.

1. Simultaneously *fondu* and *pointe tendue devant* into *rond en dehors*, finish *en fondu pointe tendue derrière*. Transfer weight without losing space between legs.
2. Return weight to front foot then pass through 1st, stretching supporting leg.

   1 – 2 (i.e. 12 bars) 12 *ronds en dehors*, the last closing 5th *derrière*.

   Repeat *en dedans*.

N.B. Use simple *ports de bras*. When *ronds* are *en dehors*, arm moves from 1st, 2nd and *bras bas* or 1st, 5th and 2nd which helps to stretch the sides of the body. For *ronds en dedans* arm moves in reverse sequence, 2nd, 5th, 1st and *bras bas*. Head must lead hand and properly used should counter-balance leg.

5 *Grands battements* transferring weight through open positions [4/4, in 2 bar phrases.]

Commence in 1st, 3rd or 5th.

2 *battements devant* at 90° closing 5th. 1 *battement devant* at 90°, closing 4th *demi-plié*, and 1 *battement derrière* to close 5th.

Repeat *derrière* and *à la 2nde*, falling into a small 2nd and moving away and towards the *barre*.

N.B. It is valuable at this point to introduce *écarté* by making the student stand diagonally to the *barre* in order to avoid kicking it on the return *à la 2nde*.

6 *Battements frappés* with transfer for spacing of large *pas marchés* [Tango in 2 bar phrases.]

Commence *sur le cou de pied*.

1. 2 *frappés devant*, the second finishing *en fondu* with *pointe tendue devant*.
2. Transfer weight *en fondu*, stretching new supporting leg and bring other *sur le cou de pied*.

Repeat in reverse and twice *à la 2nde* away and towards the *barre*. Repeat a little faster and introduce a slight spring with the transfer, seeing that the leg follows the toe down and that the supporting leg is always over its own foot.

Transfer of Weight – Intermediate *Barre*

4 *Ronds de jambe à terre* [Waltz in 4 or 6/8 in 2 bar phrases.]

Commence in 5th.

1. 2 *ronds en dehors* finishing *pointe tendue derrière*, transfer weight backwards and forwards, each time the supporting leg must sink *en fondu* very smoothly.

2 and 3. Repeat twice.

4. 1 *rond en dehors*, transfer weight backwards raising leg *devant* at 45°, transfer again to low *arabesque en fondu* (i.e. *arabesque allongée*). Close 5th *derrière*. Repeat *en dedans*.

5 *Grands battements* [Tango in 2 bar phrases.]

Commence in 5th, standing *écarté*.

1. 2 *battements devant* at 90°, closing 5th.

2. One *devant* falling into small 4th *demi-plié* and one *derrière* closing 5th *derrière*.

Repeat in reverse and *à la 2nde*, moving away and towards the *barre*. Also practise rising to *demi-pointes*, but in this case control the leg so that the supporting heel returns to the floor before the working toe reaches the surface (followed by the working heel) and only then move into *demi-plié*.

6 *Coupés ballottés* [6/8 in 2 bar phrases.]

Commence *pointe tendue derrière* with the foot next to the *barre*.

1. *Coupé, développé devant* at 45°, body slightly inclining backwards. Repeat into *coupé, développé derrière*, body moving slightly forwards.

2. *Coupé, développé à la 2nde*, body erect, and hold before *temps levé retiré devant*.

Repeat in reverse, but close 5th *demi-pointes* after opening *à la 2nde* and *détourné*, ready to repeat on other side.

Repeat, raising legs to 90°, and slightly increase the movements of the body.

Transfer of Weight – Advanced *Barre*

4 *Ronds de jambe* [Slow waltz in 4 bar phrases.]

Commence in 5th.

1. 2 *ronds en dehors* and a third passing through 1st, rising to *devant* at 90°. *Tombé en avant* to *arabesque*.

2. *Tombé en arrière*, raising leg to 90° *devant*, rise and circle *à la 2nde* at 90°. Close 5th *derrière*.

Repeat in reverse, and repeat whole.

5 *Grands battements* [Polonaise in 2 bar phrases, note timing.]

Commence in 5th.

(1) *Battement devant* at 90°. (2) Hold. (3) *Tombé* into lunge, supporting leg straight and foot flat on floor to give extra stretch.

(1) Throw leg to 90° *devant* (recovering correct stance). (2) Hold. (3) Close 5th *devant*.

Repeat *derrière* and *à la 2nde* twice.

N.B. It is essential that the head leads the movement and that the spine is kept as straight as possible when moving *devant* or *à la 2nde*, but the body must stretch appropriately into *arabesque*. The impetus for the upward throw must come from the working leg. This is to try and make students understand how much is needed to thrust the body back into its erect position.

6 *Battements frappés* and *fondus* [2/4 in 2 bar phrases; timing must be exact if the exercise is to be correct.]

Commence *sur le cou de pied*.

1. 3 *frappés à la 2nde*, finishing *sur le cou de pied*.

2. (and-a-1,) *Relevé* with *petit battement*, *fondu* and *pointe tendue devant*. (2) Hold. (and-a-3-4) Repeat *relevé*, etc. in reverse.

Repeat with *frappés doublés*.

7 *Petits battements* introducing *coupés* **[**2/4 in 2 bar phrases.**]**

Commence *sur le cou de pied*.

2 quick *petits battements* beating *derrière – devant. Coupé derrière* and hold. Feet must cut through 5th and the tip of the raised foot be fully stretched over the ankle bone.

Repeat in reverse.

Repeat 4 times in all and then faster, using small *fondu* as toe reaches floor during *coupé*.

N.B. Do not allow hips to 'rock', this is not a hornpipe.

46 Florestan's *fouetté sauté,* from *The Sleeping Beauty* (Phillip Broomhead): *a* the preparatory jump upwards;

b the turn in the air before the descent

8 *Adage* Slow *battements fondus* with transfer through the centre **[**Slow tango or habanera in 4 bar phrases.**]**

Commence in 3rd or 5th.

Coupé devant en fondu, stretch supporting leg and other to 20° or 45° *devant* (see note below), transfer weight through *demi-pointes* and stretch *derrière* at same height. Transfer weight through *demi-pointes* and stretch *à la 2nde* at same height. Close 5th *devant sur demi-pointes* and *détourné*.

Repeat on other side and then again, raising leg to 45° or 90°.

N.B. When practising these *battements fondus*, the upper leg, when bent, should be held as still as possible and at the correct height for the following stretch: if the stretch is to 20° the tips of the toes rest on the ankle bone, if to 45° on the bottom of the calf and if to 90° at mid-calf or higher. They can also be held at knee level if the student is expected to stretch or bend the body slightly backwards when *devant*, into *arabesque* and sideways to the *barre* when *à la 2nde*. Such accuracy of placing helps the student to sustain the smooth and equal stretch of both legs. Similarly the *ports de bras* must be smooth and controlled. Ensure that the supporting leg stretches fully before any rise is attempted.

Transfer of Weight – Intermediate *Barre*

7 *Petits battements* into *pirouettes en dehors* and *en dedans* [2/4 in 2 bar phrases.]

Commence *sur le cou de pied*.

2 *petits battements*, close 5th *devant demi-plié* and immediately *relevé – retiré* into *pirouette en dehors*. During the *pirouette* the *retiré* should come *derrière* and finish *sur le cou de pied derrière* as the supporting leg sinks *en fondu*.

Repeat in reverse with *pirouette en dedans*. (Do not use *fouetté*). Repeat 4 times in all.

N.B. The feet must close tightly together in *demi-plié* and the working foot must be drawn up the side to the front or back of the supporting leg as the turn begins. The student should be encouraged to work absolutely *en place*.

8 *Adage* [Slow minuet in 4 bar phrases or sarabande.]

Commence in 5th.

1. *Développé devant* at 90° or above with slight backward bend of upper torso and head, arms 2nd; *tombé* into *arabesque allongée*, arms to *arabesque*.
2. Stretch supporting leg whilst holding *arabesque*, rise on *demi-pointes*, hold and close 5th *derrière*.

Repeat in reverse and *à la 2nde*, moving away and towards the *barre*, changing the *épaulement* to *écarté*.

N.B. Ensure that the body follows the toe downwards, that the head leads the movement and that as far as possible hips and shoulders remain parallel and facing the same plane. Do NOT allow any twisting. The change of *épaulement* should only be seen by the turn of the head over the shoulder into the *tombé* and in the way the body is at an angle to the *barre*.

Transfer of Weight – Advanced *Barre*

7 *Relevés* with *petits ronds* into *attitude* [Waltz in 4 bar phrases.]

Commence in 5th.

Relevé into *battement à la 2nde* at 45° (or 90°), 2 *petits ronds doublés en l'air en dehors*; *retiré en fondu* and *relevé* into *attitude devant*. Close 5th *devant*.

Repeat in reverse. Then repeat whole.

N.B. There must be simultaneous movement into *retiré en fondu* and the *relevé* into *attitude*.

8 *Adage* [Slow minuet, waltz or sarabande in 4 bar phrases.]

Commence in 5th.

1. *Développé devant en fondu*, transfer to *arabesque*, rise and rotate to *devant* at 90°, *grand rond de jambe en dehors*.
2. Step back and raise leg to 90° *devant*, rotate to *arabesque*, *grand rond de jambe en dedans* and hold *devant* at 90°.

N.B. Ensure that the hips do not twist and that the weight remains always centred over the supporting leg during the rotations. Also ensure that working toe is in line with supporting heel – this will help to keep body in correct alignment.

47   *Grand jeté en attitude,* from *Napoli* (Stephen Sherriff)

Transfer of Weight – Elementary *Barre*

9 Exercise as an introduction for *grands jetés en avant* [3/4 in 4 bar phrases.]

Commence in 5th.

Coupé devant en fondu, rise and simultaneously stretch leg *devant* with spine and head upwards and slightly backwards. Do not raise leg any higher than 90°. Breathe in and following the line of the leg downwards *tombé* into *arabesque fondue.* The line should trace a curve upwards, over and down. Breathe out and close 5th *derrière.*

Repeat in reverse, and the whole 4 times in all.

N.B. It is absolutely essential to control the first opening of the leg and the whole body must be seen to travel over and forwards.

Transfer of Weight – Elementary Centre

1 (*Petit adage*) [Steady 2/4 in 4 bar phrases, accent is up and down on beat to give correct impetus.]

Commence in 5th *croisé.*

  1. 2 *tendus devant,* the second closing 5th *demi-plié, pointe tendue,* transfer weight forwards, backwards and forwards, close 5th.
  2. Repeat *derrière.*
  3. Repeat *à la 2nde.*
  4. *Glissade dessous, glissade dessus, échappé* into small 4th and *pirouette en dehors,* finishing on opposite side 5th *devant,* ready to repeat on other side.

Transfer of Weight – Intermediate *Barre*

9 Practice for *grands jetés* [6/8 in 2 bar phrases.]

Repeat as for Ex. 9, page 88, in Elementary Transfer of Weight, but after *coupé* simultaneously rise on *demi-pointe* and *développé devant,* then spring lightly forwards and hold *arabesque en fondu* before closing in 5th.

Repeat in reverse.

N.B. The height of the raised leg, the slight arching of the back and the placing of the weight of the body firstly on the supporting leg and then, after the transfer, on the other must all be firmly controlled.

Transfer of Weight – Intermediate Centre

1 (*Petit adage*) For the spacing of steps, i.e. the need for concentration on the space to be covered in any one movement [3/4 in 4 bar phrases.]

Commence *croisé, effacé* or *de face* and move either diagonally or straight forwards.

1. *Chassé en avant* on straight legs, rise, lower heels, close 5th *derrière* (or *devant*, depending on which way the dancer travels).
2. *Demi-plié, chassé en avant* to *pointe tendue derrière,* i.e. space for *échappés sur les pointes.* Transfer and straighten new supporting knee, i.e. normal sized step for *pas marché.*
3. Simultaneously *fondu* and *pointe tendue devant,* transfer through large *demi-plié,* closing and straightening new supporting leg, i.e. largest space when transferring *à terre.*
4. *Sissonne ordinaire* into *chassé assemblé porté en avant, échappé* into small 4th and *pirouette en dedans,* i.e. the largest space should be covered *à terre* when impetus is given by a slight jump upwards and a full stretch outwards of the working leg when in the air, as well as the impetus given by the weight of the body also being stretched into the direction to be travelled.

This must be practised moving backwards and sideways, always trying to make the students understand the need to travel the same distance no matter which way they move.

Transfer of Weight – Advanced *Barre*

9 Practice for transfer of weight from *relevés* and *tombés* [Mazurka in 2 bar phrases, note timing.]

Commence in 5th.

(1) Simultaneously *relevé* and *développé devant* above 90° with slight backward stretch of upper torso and head. (2) Hold. (3) *Tombé* into *arabesque allongée.* (1) Hold. (2) *Relevé* into *arabesque.* (3) Hold. (anacrusis) Lower heel.

(1) *Relevé* into *arabesque* (2) Hold. (3) *Tombé en arrière.*

(1) *Relevé* into *attitude devant.* (2) Hold. (3) Close 5th *devant.*

Repeat *à la 2nde* away and towards the *barre* and then *derrière.*

N.B. Use conventional *ports de bras* and ensure that neither hips nor shoulders twist during the *tombés* and *relevés.*

Transfer of Weight – Advanced Centre

1 (*Petit adage*) [5/4 very steady. Please note timing.]

Commence in 5th *croisé.*

(1) *Pointe tendue devant.* (2) Drop heel. (3) Re-point toe. (4) Circle *à la 2nde.* (5) Drop heel.

(1) Using other foot, *pointe tendue à la 2nde.* (2) Drop heel. (3) Re-point toe. (4) Close 5th *derrière.* (5) Quick *battement tendu à la 2nde,* closing 5th *derrière.*

(1) *Pointe tendue devant.* (2) Close. (3) Make half turn *en dehors* (i.e. to back corner) to *pointe tendue à la 2nde.* (4) Close 5th *derrière.* (5) Make quarter turn to *pointe tendue derrière.*

(1) Close 5th *derrière.* (2) Circle front foot to *pointe tendue derrière* (i.e. dancer is now *effacé*). (3) Drop to small 4th *demi-plié.* (4) *Pirouette en dehors.* (5) Finish 5th *derrière,* ready to repeat on other side.

48   The Firebird flies through the magic garden, from *The Firebird* (Fiona Chadwick)

2 (*Petit adage*) [Waltz in 4 bar phrases.]

Commence in 5th *de face*.

1. *Glissades en avant* and *en arrière*, stretch knees and 2 *ronds en dehors à terre*, closing 5th *devant*.
2. Repeat in reverse, using other foot, i.e. *en dedans*.
3. *Pointe tendue devant*, drop heel and transfer weight forwards and backwards, close 5th *devant*.
4. *Pointe tendue devant*, circle *derrière* to small 4th *demi-plié* and *pirouette en dehors*, finishing 5th *derrière*, ready to repeat on other side.

3 (*Grand adage*) *ADAGE*: Slow *temps lié* [6/8, dance very smoothly and do NOT hold any pose or pause on *demi-pointe* during transfer.]

Commence in 5th *croisé*.

Fondu into *retiré*, arms 1st, and *développé devant*, arms to open 4th; transfer weight to 3rd *arabesque*. *Coupé de face*, arms 1st, and *développé à la 2nde*, arms 4th; transfer weight, lifting other leg *à la 2nde*, and change arms over head to 4th, close 5th *devant bras bas* and change *épaulement*, ready to repeat on other side.

4 *Pirouettes en dedans* with and without *fouetté* movement

Repeat as for Balance (page 76) but make one complete turn *en relevé*.

N.B. It is absolutely essential to fix the weight firmly over the supporting leg when opening to *pointe tendue*. In this way all forces will be drawn together. Then simultaneously *fondu* and drop the working heel for the *relevé* into the *pirouette*.

2 (*Petit adage*) With concentration on the exact direction to be taken [Waltz in 2 bar phrases.]

Commence in 5th *croisé*.

1. 1 *rond en dehors en fondu* to *pointe tendue derrière*, make exact half turn and step forwards on to 5th *demi-pointes*.
2. Repeat with *rond en dedans* and step forwards into original corner.
3. *Grand battement devant* finishing small 4th; *grand battement derrière*, closing 5th *derrière*.
4. *Grand battement à la 2nde* finishing in small 2nd *demi-plié* as preparation for *pirouette en dehors*, finishing 5th *devant*.

3 (*Grand adage*) ADAGE [6/8 in 2 bar phrases.]

Commence in 5th *croisé*.

1. Rise and *développé devant* sinking *en fondu*, circle to *écarté devant* then *tombé* with *ports de bras* sideways. (i.e. the now supporting leg will be *en fondu*, other in *pointe tendue*) recover balance in *écarté devant*.
2. Circle to *attitude effacée*, *voyagé* into *attitude croisée* (turn towards supporting leg) and stretch into *pas de basque en arrière* into 1st *arabesque* (i.e. on third step lift leg into *arabesque*).
3. 2 *pas marchés en arrière* into 1st *arabesque* (i.e. lift leg on second step).
4. Sweep through 1st to *devant* at 90° and *tombé* into *pirouette en dedans en attitude*. Hold. Repeat after pause.

4 *Pirouettes* from *échappés* (Particularly useful for boys) [Strong waltz in 2 bar phrases; students must anticipate beat and land from *échappé* on 1st beat.]

1. *Echappé changé* into 4th *demi-plié* on other side and immediately into *pirouette en dehors* (pick up back foot), finishing 5th *derrière*.
2. Repeat on other side.
3. *Echappé* into 4th, weight over front foot, and *pirouette en dedans*, finishing 4th *devant* on other side. Immediately into *pirouette en dehors* (pick up back foot), finishing 4th *derrière demi-plié*.
4. Another *pirouette en dehors*, finishing 5th *derrière*, ready to repeat on other side.

2 (*Petit adage*) [Waltz in 4 bar phrases.]

Commence in 5th *croisé*.

1. *Rond de jambe en dehors en fondu*, stretch supporting leg and pass through 1st to 2 quick *ronds* finishing *pointe tendue devant*.
2. *Fondu* on front leg, dropping back heel, *pirouette en dedans* finishing 4th *devant demi-plié* and immediately into *pirouette en dehors* (i.e. pick up back foot), ready to repeat on other side.

Go straight into *pirouette en dedans* without *fouetté*.

3 (*Grand adage*) ADAGE [Sarabande or minuet in 2 bar phrases.]

Commence in 5th *croisé*.

1. *Chassé en avant* to *pointe tendue derrière*, arms 5th, transfer weight backwards and raise leg *devant* to 90° *à deux bras*.
2. Pass through 1st to 2nd *arabesque* and rotate *en dehors* to *attitude croisée*.
3. Stretch into *arabesque* and turning backwards 2 running steps and *saut de basque* finishing *retiré effacé*, *développé devant*.
4. *Grand rond de jambe en dehors* and *tombé* into 4th *effacé*, *pirouette en dedans*, finishing *pointe tendue devant*. Pause before repeating on other side.

4 *Pirouettes* [6/8, an eight bar phrase only.]

Commence in 5th *croisé*.

1. *Pointe tendue devant* with the right foot into small 4th *demi-plié*, *pirouette en dehors* finishing *pointe tendue devant* with the left foot.
2. Pass left foot through 1st and *posé en arrière* in low *arabesque*, *fondu* sinking into 4th and *pirouette en dedans*, finishing *à la 2nde* at 90° *de face*, arms 4th.
3. *Pas de bourrée dessus* into small 4th and *pirouette en dehors en attitude devant* (pick up back foot).
4. Hold then stretch foot *pas marché en avant*, closing 5th *sur demi-* or full *pointes*.

N.B. During this last *pirouette* the same arm should be raised into closed 4th as leg in front. It must move into position immediately the turn begins. The stretch of the head and upper torso is all important.

49 *Ballottés coupés* (Karen Paisey):
a ballotté devant;
b coupé (posed *à terre* to
demonstrate exact position);
c ballotté derrière

Transfer of Weight – Elementary Centre

5 (*Petit allegro*) [*A six temps* or 3 strong beats in 2 bar phrases.]
Commence in 5th *croisé*.
1. *Pas de basque glissé en dehors, pas de bourrée piqué dessous.*
2. Repeat.
3. *Pas de basque glissé en dedans, 3 soubresauts en avant.*
4. *Coupé devant, assemblé dessous, changement*, ready to repeat on other side.

6 (*Petit allegro*) [Waltz in 2 bar phrases.]
Commence *pointe tendue croisé derrière*.
1. *Demi-contretemps* changing *épaulement* into *assemblé porté écarté* to 5th *devant*, arms moving from 3rd to 1st and open 4th.
2. *Failli, glissade derrière*, i.e. *failli* means both feet leave the floor at the same time so that the *glissade* begins from 4th, arms move from 1st to 2nd.
3. *Pas de chat, pas de bourrée dessous*, arms 5th to 3rd.
4. *Sissonne fermée dessus* and open to *pointe tendue derrière*, ready to repeat on other side.

N.B. It is very important to distinguish between *failli* and *demi-contretemps*. The *failli* must start with a jump upwards and slightly sideways with both feet; the front leg then descends, the back leg passing through 1st to 4th, usually with a change of *épaulement*. *Demi-contretemps* starts from an open position and a spring off the supporting leg, the other held in low *arabesque*. The working leg then passes through 1st to 4th, also with a change of *épaulement*, and weight then transferred to the front foot.

7 (*Grand allegro*) [Grand waltz in 4 bar phrases.]
Commence *effacé pointe tendue devant* ready to move *en diagonale*.
1. *Pas de bourrée* into *grand jeté en avant* and repeat.
2. 4 *balancés* (or *pas de valse*) moving straight backwards, ready to repeat *grands jetés* from other side.

N.B. Use opposition arms for *grands jetés* and do not use 'flick' or 'split' *jetés*. This is the classical *grand jeté* and must go up, over and down. See Ex. 9 , page 88.

5 (*Petit allegro*) [Easy waltz in 4 bar phrases.]

Commence in 5th *de face*.

1. *Pas de chat, pas de bourrée dessus*, 2 *brisés dessous*.
2. Repeat on other side.
3. *Failli, glissade derrière, temps de cuisse*.
4. *Assemblé dessus, pas de bourrée en tournant en dehors, entrechat quatre*, ready to repeat on other side.

6 (*Petit allegro*) [6/8 in 2 bar phrases.]

Commence in 5th *de face*.

1. *Soubresaut, temps levé derrière, assemblé derrière, entrechat trois derrière*.
2. *Assemblé dessus*, 2 *brisés en avant, changement battu*, ready to repeat on other side.

7 (*Grand allegro*) [Tango in 2 bar phrases.]

Commence *pointe tendue effacé devant*.

Posé into 1st *arabesque* passing through 1st into large 4th and *assemblé porté dessus*. Hold before repeating 4 times in all.

N.B. The body must be *de face* to the corner in *arabesque* and move to *écarté* for the *assemblé* and finish in 5th if the line of the step is to be understood.

5 (*Petit allegro*) [2/4 steady in 2 bar phrases.]

Commence in 5th *de face*.

1. *Glissade dessus* and *glissade dessous, entrechat quatre, entrechat six*.
2. Repeat on other side.
3. 2 *sissonnes dessus, glissade en arrière, entrechat quatre*.
4. 2 *sissonnes dessous, glissade en avant, entrechat six*.

N.B. It is essential that all *glissades* close in strong 5th *demi-pliés* as preparation for the *entrechats*.

6 (*Petit allegro*) [2/4 in 2 bar phrases.]

Commence in 5th *écarté*.

1. 2 *brisés en avant, glissade* and *petit jeté derrière*.
2. *Temps levé* into *attitude croisée, temps levé* stretching into *arabesque* and turning into 2 running steps, *assemblé battu devant*, ready to repeat on other side.

7 (*Grand allegro*) [Steady waltz in 4 bar phrases.]

Commence in 5th *écarté*.

1. *Sauté ballonné écarté*, i.e. spring slightly backwards raising leg *à la 2nde* at 90° before cutting it back to *retiré derrière, jeté élancé en arrière, assemblé devant, temps levé à la 2nde*, into:
2. *Pas de bourrée en tournant en dedans* into *grand rond de jambe sauté en dehors* (use full *rond de jambe* before bending leg into *attitude*) and into *pas de bourrée en tournant en dehors*, closing 5th *devant. Changement*, ready to repeat on other side. (See page 105, Ex. 3.)

8 *Pirouettes posées en dedans en diagonale* **[2/4.]**

Commence as set out on page 67.

Step forwards on a *demi-pointe* (or full *pointe*) bring left foot into *retiré devant* (or *derrière*), thus completing one turn, *coupé* and repeat this movement in series.

N.B. The head must anticipate the line to be travelled, the eyes focus on the same 'spot' in the opposite corner with each turn. The arms and shoulders must be absolutely controlled. It is usual to practise these turns firstly with *retiré derrière* as this helps to maintain turn-out. But they should also be practised with *retiré devant*.

9 *Ports de bras* **[Minuet in 4 bar phrases.]**

Commence in 5th *croisé, bras bas*.

1. *Chassé en avant* to *pointe tendue derrière*, arms 1st to 4th; bend forwards, transferring weight to back foot, arms 3rd to 3rd at moment of transfer; transfer weight forwards, stretching body and head, arms 4th to 4th. (The body must only bend forwards and backwards as the arms change – never through 1st.) Close 5th.

2. Repeat 1.

3. *Chassé en avant* as before but circle left arm to 2nd, *bras bas* and up to 4th whilst transferring weight backwards and circling body slightly forwards from left to right before arms stretch up to 4th; transfer weight forwards again changing arms 4th to 4th, then through 1st and back to original position.

4. *Fondu*, stretching body and bending it forwards thus lengthening the line into *pointe tendue derrière*, whilst still bending forwards raise both arms to 5th; stretch to 3rd *arabesque à terre*. Stretch body upwards and circle working leg *en dedans* to close 5th *devant*, arms 2nd to 3rd; 2 *pas de bourrée dessous*, changing *épaulement* and finishing 5th, opening arms to 2nd and *bras bas*, ready to repeat on other side.

Transfer of Weight – Intermediate Centre

8 *Pirouettes chassées en tournant en diagonale* [Gallop.]

Commence in 5th *effacé* or *de face* to the direction to be travelled.

Chassé en avant with sufficient impetus to make one full turn by the time the other foot closes 5th *derrière*. (Turn takes place *en l'air* but not far from the floor. The tips of the toes should only just leave the surface.) Continue in series. Arms move from 3rd to 1st in as small a movement as possible. The impetus comes from the leading foot and the shoulder coming into the turn.

9 *Emboîtés* [2/4.]

Although these are sometimes taught as *petits jetés en tournant*, they must be more carefully placed and the thrust of the leg outwards as the other is brought into *retiré* must be well controlled and not widely spaced. The legs should be brought inwards and under the body.

Commence in 5th *écarté*, head and eyes directed to the other corner. Spring slightly forwards making a half turn whilst bringing the other leg *retiré devant*, repeat by springing slightly forwards on the other foot making another half turn, other leg *retiré* (thus completing one full turn). Continue to repeat in series.

N.B. The spring upwards into the half turn must be simultaneous with the *retiré*. It is most important to get this simultaneous action if the turn is to be neat. The toe should reach at least mid-calf. This helps to indicate the height of the little spring. A higher spring, unless needed by a choreographer, is not advisable. The tighter the *retiré*, the neater the turn and thus more *jetés* will cover the space allowed. This is most important when dancing at speed. Keep the arms under firm control. They scarcely need to move at all unless the movements are slow.

Transfer of Weight – Advanced Centre

8 *Pirouettes* opening *à la 2nde* at 90° *en diagonale* [Steady waltz.]

Commence *pointe tendue devant*, etc. (see page 96)

Step forwards to corner on right foot and simultaneously circle left foot forwards, then step on to full *pointe*. Whilst making the full turn, lift right leg through *retiré* to *développé à la 2nde*, holding pose momentarily before falling on to right foot. Take another step forwards on the left with half turn and another step right, ready to repeat *posé* turn with *développé à la 2nde*. Continue on in series.

N.B. Because the head must be turned over the leading shoulder and the arms open to 4th on the *développé*, the dancer must hold the position *écarté* when the leg opens.

9 When mastered *en diagonale*, **8** should be practised *en manège*. As in all *pirouettes posées*, the supporting leg, torso and head must be strictly controlled so that the dancer is seen *écarté* when the pose is held momentarily. It is also essential that the *tombé* after the turn before the *pas marché* (or step) is not too large because the two little steps should seem to be all but *en place*.

Boys should also practise this, commencing with *balancé en tournant*, i.e. right, left, right, then springing forwards and round to make a three-quarter turn on the left foot whilst bringing the right leg through *retiré* to *développé écarté*, then continue in series.

Rules

PRINCIPLES

'It is better to have a rule to break than no rule at all if discipline is to be maintained in the class-room.' Ninette de Valois.

These final classes attempt to cover all aspects of the Principles studied earlier and to follow the Rules laid down by the great masters. These were no better codified than by Dame Ninette during her yearly courses for teachers which followed the opening in 1947 of what is now the Royal Ballet School. Only by following the Principles and Rules will students learn to co-ordinate their understanding of their own bodies with their technical knowledge and thus produce a musical and artistic performance of classical dance.

RULES

A The head must always move freely and independently, turning, inclining or bending forwards, backwards or sideways to counter-balance and/or stabilise the movements of arms, body and legs. It must always be stretched upwards and away from the cervical vertebrae.

Another important function of the eyes must be encouraged in these classes. This is the use of what is called 'wide vision'. That is, the student must be taught to experience a wide view of the stage and not only to focus on a particular 'spot', which is so necessary in steps such as *pirouettes*. From the centre back of the studio, it should be possible to see at a single glance everything to the right and left as well as the parts of ceiling and floor in front of the dancer. It is only by cultivating this 'wide vision' that the dancer will be able to visualise the patterns danced on stage, a room from which one wall has been removed and replaced by what on first entrance appears as a large, black, empty space. Yet the audience is there and must be acknowledged. This can only be done if the dancer's eyes and head are ready to make that greeting.

B The arms should never touch the body, the finger-tips never meet and neither arms nor legs should ever over- or under-cross, because they must counter-balance each other. The arms must always be rounded except in *arabesque*.

In both Intermediate and Advanced classes throughout my series I give *enchaînements* for varied turning steps *en diagonale* or *en manège* in both of which the correct use of the head is vital. I have found it essential to concentrate on its natural (see photos 50a and b, 51, 52, 53, 54a and b)

1 *Pliés* as practice for jumps
Repeat as for Laws of Balance (page 68).

2 *Battements tendus* with quickening tempos.
Repeat as for Elementary Ex. **2** page 68 but rise on *demi-pointes* during the first slow *tendu* and close the second quick one in *demi-plié*.

ability to turn directly from side to side independently of neck and shoulders. It can circle half way round and then return whilst the body makes a full turn. Thus I encourage students to start *pointe tendue devant* to a front, head turned directly over the leading shoulder (i.e. *écarté*), eyes focused on a 'spot' whilst making a half turn, then immediately turn it back over the leading shoulder to complete the *pirouette*. It is for this reason that I prefer to teach *pirouettes enchaînées* (*déboulés*) before others when attempting to travel across or round the studio. I find it easier to explain the idea of turning the head on each transfer of weight (or step) during a half turn.

As in any turning step the arms must be kept under strict control. The leading arm must not stretch out to a full 2nd or move behind the shoulder and the incoming arm must meet it in a shortened 1st simultaneously with the beginning of the turn. Moreover the arms in 1st position should be level with the bottom of the breast bone, never higher if the shoulders are to be held downwards, thus leaving the head to move freely and the breathing not to be impaired.

FOCAL POINTS

1. The hip line (page 5).
2. The foot (page 5).
3. Upper torso (page 6).
4. The head (page 10).

Rules – Intermediate *Barre*

1 *Pliés*

Repeat as for Ex. **1**. page 69.

2 *Battements tendus* to establish small and large positions [4/4 in 2 bar phrases.]
Commence in 5th.

Chassé en avant to small 4th (i.e. merely slide whole foot forwards on floor), rise, lower heels and slide foot backwards to 5th. Raise arms to 1st *arabesque* during the slide forwards. *Pointe tendue devant* closing 5th *demi-plié*, *chassé en avant*, and, transferring weight, stretch both legs to rest *pointe tendue derrière*, close 5th. Repeat in reverse and *à la 2nde* away and towards the *barre*.

N.B. First *chassé* is very small on straight legs, the second *chassé* is a normal *pas marché* so that the weight is always correctly centred.

Rules – Advanced *Barre*

1 Repeat as Ex. **1** for Stance (see page 27).

2 *Battements tendus* as preparation for landing from jumps [4/4 in 2 bar phrases.]
Commence in 5th.

1. 2 *tendus devant*, the second closing *sur le cou de pied*, simultaneously *fondu* and *pointe tendue devant*, transfer weight forwards *en fondu* stretching to *pointe tendue derrière*, transfer again to back foot and close 5th, stretching knees.
2 – 3. Repeat *à la 2nde* and *derrière*.
4. 2 *tendus à la 2nde*, the second closing 5th *demi-plié devant*, *glissades en avant* and *en arrière*, *détourné*, ready to repeat on other side.

N.B. It is essential to retain weight over supporting leg *en fondu* and to stretch the working leg to its fullest as well as to retain the depth of the *fondu* as the weight is transferred.

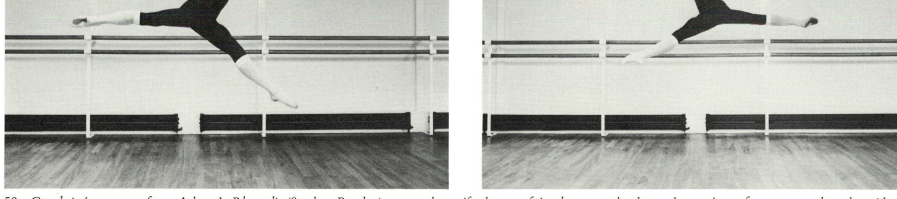

50 *Grands jetés en avant,* from Ashton's *Rhapsodie* (Stephen Beagley) – note the swift change of *épaulement* as the dancer has to jump from one to the other side without preparation: *a* to the right; *b* to the left

3 *Battements glissés* both slow and quick [2/4 in 2 bar phrases.]

Repeat as for Exercise **3** page 68, but perform *sur demi-pointes* closing the second quick one in *demi-plié* and make sure that feet close tightly each time so that weight is momentarily over both.

4 *Ronds de jambe* as practice for *pas de basque* [3/4 in 4 bar phrases.]

Commence in 1st, 3rd or 5th.

1. 3 quarter *ronds en dehors* circling *devant* – *à la 2nde* and 1st and fourth full *rond* closing 1st.
2. Repeat *en dehors*, circling *à la 2nde*, *derrière* and 1st and fourth full *rond* closing 1st.
3 – 4. Repeat whole, moving *en dedans*.

Repeat 4 times in all.

5 *Grands battements* to *pointes piquées* [4/4 in 2 bar phrases.]

Commence in 3rd or 5th.

Battement devant to 90°, finishing *pointe piquée devant*, repeat, closing 3rd or 5th. Repeat whole.

Repeat *en croix*. Raise arm to 5th for *battements devant* and *à la 2nde* and *arabesque* for *derrière*.

51 *Temps de poisson*, from the Bluebirds' *pas de deux, The Sleeping Beauty* (Stephen Beagley)

3 *Battements glissés* as practice for landing from jumps [Tarantella in 2 bar phrases.]

Commence in 5th.

1. 2 *glissés devant* and, simultaneously with the third, raise leg *glissé* to 20° and hold.
2. With a slight spring, transfer weight forwards, backwards and forwards (i.e. three changes) before closing 5th.

N.B. During each change of weight the working leg must rise cleanly from the floor, fully stretched, whilst the supporting one sinks *en fondu*. Repeat, moving *derrière* and *à la 2nde* away and towards the *barre*, ensuring that at no time the hips and shoulders twist. They must be kept level and always facing the same plane.

4 *Ronds de jambe* with *développés* [Slow waltz in 4 bar phrases.]

Commence in 5th.

1. *Développé devant* at 90°, drop to *pointe tendue devant* and close 5th. Repeat *développé à la 2nde*, closing 5th *derrière*.
2. Repeat with *développé derrière*, dropping to *pointe tendue derrière*, pass through 1st and into 2 *ronds en dehors*.
3. 4 *ronds en dehors*, arms from 1st to 5th, 2nd and *bras bas*.
4. 1 slow *rond en dehors en fondu*, close 5th *derrière* and rise on *demi-pointes*.

Repeat whole *en dedans*.

5 *Grands battements* [March in 2 bar phrases, up on first beat.]

Commence in 5th.

1. *Battement devant* at 90°, finishing *pointe tendue devant en fondu*. Throw leg upwards, with the supporting leg stretched, and finish *retiré devant en fondu*.
2. Repeat, closing 5th *demi-plié*, and repeat again, closing 5th with straight legs.

Repeat *derrière* and twice *à la 2nde*.

N.B. Ensure that the hips and shoulders remain facing the same plane throughout and that the weight remains at all times centred fully over the supporting leg. Therefore, ensure that the working leg is always controlled, as it is easier to throw the leg higher when *en fondu*.

3 *Battements glissés* as further practice for landing from jumps [Tarantella in 2 bar phrases.]

2 *glissés devant* and, simultaneously with the third, *fondu* and hold. Transfer weight forwards, backwards and forwards, close 5th *derrière*.

N.B. Use a slight spring on to new supporting leg during the transfer but keep hips and shoulders level and facing the same plane during the *fondu*. Also compare with the *battements tendus* above. In the former the movement should seem to be glided along the surface of the floor, whilst the latter should be seen to be jumped over it. (See page 97.)

4 *Ronds de jambe* with *grands ronds jetés* [Slow waltz in 4 bar phrases.]

Commence in 5th.

1. 2 *ronds en dehors* pass through 1st to *attitude devant en fondu*, throw leg upwards *à la 2nde* and circle to *arabesque*. The supporting leg must be fully stretched as the other reaches its highest point *à la 2nde* and must sink into *fondu* again as *arabesque* is reached.
2 – 3. Repeat 1 twice before stretching to *pointe tendue derrière*.
4. Move into *grand ports de bras*. Recover to repeat *en dedans*.

N.B. Supporting and working legs must stretch upwards simultaneously and the arm rise from 1st to 5th at the same moment before moving to *arabesque* with open 5th. Please compare this *rond* with that on page 45.

5 *Grands battements* using cross rhythms [Polonaise in 2 bar phrases and accenting 1st, 3rd and 5th beats.]

Commence in 5th.

1. 3 *grands battements devant*.
2. 3 *grands battements derrière*.
3. 3 *grands battements à la 2nde*.
4. *Relevé* to *attitude devant* and hold; pass through *retiré* to *attitude*, arm in open 5th. Close and repeat *sur les pointes*.

52 *Jeté élancé en écarté*, from Ashton's *Rhapsodie* (Stephen Beagley) – note that the dancer has to travel all but along the floor

6 *Battements frappés* as practice for *assemblés* [Slow 2/4 in 2 bar phrases.]

2 *frappés devant* with strong accent outwards. Close 5th *demi-plié* and spring into *assemblé devant en place*. Immediately lift *sur le cou de pied devant* and repeat *à la 2nde* with *assemblé dessus*. Repeat in reverse.

N.B. The *assemblé* must be *en place*. To ensure this, the supporting leg must spring upwards only, with the fully stretched working leg leaving the floor and then brought back to the other on the descent into *demi-plié*.

7 *Petits battements* as an introduction to a single *pirouette* [3/4.]

Commence *sur le cou de pied*.

Repeat as No.7 page 70 but use a single turn for *pirouette*.

Repeat 4 times in all turning *en dehors*. Then repeat, turning *en dedans* and moving straight into the *retiré* without *fouetté* (see page 70).

8 *Adage* [3/4 in 4 bar or 6/8 in 3 bar phrases, or sarabande.]

Commence in 3rd or 5th.

This is an introduction to *grand rond de jambe*, so the working leg must be held at 45°, no higher, until balance is stable.

Développé devant, circle *à la 2nde* and to *arabesque*. Close 5th *derrière*. Then *ports de bras* before repeating *en dedans*.

N.B. Ensure that the weight is always sustained over the supporting leg, that the hips do not twist, and that the supporting arm moves very slightly forwards as the leg circles behind and returns to its correct place as the leg returns to side. The students will find it helpful if they breathe in at the moment of leaving side and just as their leg leaves back on the return. The intake of breath helps to slim the waist by expanding the rib-cage and this takes the weight upwards and centres it firmly over the supporting leg. Use conventional *ports de bras*.

Rules – Intermediate *Barre*

6 *Battements frappés* into *petits ronds de jambe en l'air* [2/4 in 2 bar phrases.]

Commence *sur le cou de pied*.

1. 4 *frappés à la 2nde*, on the fourth raise leg to 75°.
2. 3 *petits ronds de jambe en l'air en dehors*, close *sur le cou de pied derrière*, ready to repeat using *petits ronds en dedans*.

Repeat, using a *relevé* on the fourth *frappé* and hold on *demi-pointe* during the *ronds*.

Later repeat with *ronds doublés*.

7 *Petits battements* into *pirouettes*, finishing *en attitude*

Repeat as for Intermediate Ex.7 page 87 but more slowly and finish each *pirouette en dehors en attitude* and each *pirouette en dedans en attitude devant*. Each pose should be held on *demi-* or full *pointe*.

N.B. It is essential that the hand does not grasp the *barre* until the *pirouette* is finished and the *attitude* held. The purpose of the exercise is to ensure that the *pirouette* finishes on the *demi-* or full *pointe*. This is valuable practice for girls attempting double-work, particularly supported *adage*, when they must rely on the strength of their 'muscular corset' and not only on the boys' hands to stop the turn.

8 *Adage*: very slow *coupés ballottés* at 90° with bends of the body [6/8 in 2 bar phrases.]

Commence *pointe tendue derrière* (i.e. with the foot next to the *barre*).

1. *Coupé développé ballotté en avant* passing through 5th *demi-pointes* and curving body well backwards, arm to 4th; *coupé ballotté derrière* passing through 5th *demi-pointes* and bending slightly forwards, arm 2nd (i.e. body should be *penchée*).
2. *Coupé ballotté à la 2nde*, arm 4th and bending slightly towards the *barre*. Close 5th *devant demi-pointes* and *détourné*.

Repeat on other side, and then repeat all.

Rules – Advanced *Barre*

6 Practice for *pointes* [2/4.]

Commence in 5th.

(and-1) *Relevé retiré devant* and *fondu* to *pointe tendue devant*. (and-2, and-3) Repeat twice. (and-4) *Relevé* with *petit battement sur le cou de pied* to *pointe tendue derrière*.

Repeat *derrière*, finishing *pointe tendue à la 2nde*.

Repeat *à la 2nde*, finishing *relevé retiré devant* and close 5th. (and-1, and-2, and-3) 3 *relevés retirés passés*. (4) Hold ready to repeat in reverse.

Later repeat, using changes of *épaulement*, either *effacé* or *croisé*.

7 *Coupés ballottés* [6/8.]

Repeat as for Ex.6 on page 85 but dance *sur les pointes* and with well stretched *ports de bras*, the body bending well backwards, arm 5th when *devant* (it should be over 90°) and falling into well stretched *arabesque allongée* and then towards the *barre* when *à la 2nde*.

N.B. The movement must appear free but be completely controlled so that the HOLD at the last moment of the stretch can be clearly seen as a definite pose.

8 *Adage*: practice for *grand rond de jambe renversé* [Slow waltz in 4 bar phrases.]

Commence in 5th.

Fondu, lifting working leg to open *attitude devant*, arm 1st, stretch and rise on supporting leg whilst working leg opens *devant*, circles *à la 2nde* arm stretching to 5th, and continue to circle to *arabesque*. Immediately *arabesque* is reached, *fondu* and bend the working leg into *attitude* and the body sideways to the *barre*. At this moment begin to turn *en dehors*, stretching legs, body and head upwards closing 5th *derrière sur les pointes* and into *pas de bourrée piqué en dehors*. The arm moves from 2nd to *bras bas* and 1st as the dancer turns (i.e. the foot closing 5th is the first step of the *bourrée*).

Repeat 4 times in all, then repeat on the other side.

N.B. It is essential to complete a full *rond* before bending into *attitude fondue*, as well as to see the stretch upwards *à la 2nde*. When joining the feet together in 5th, the body should have turned a quarter and is now upright.

Rules – Elementary *Barre*

9 Preparation for *glissades sur les pointes* [2/4.]

Commence in 5th facing and with both hands on the *barre*.

(and-1) *relevé sur les pointes*, step sideways on to right *pointe* on fully stretched leg before joining left to it in 5th *devant*.

(and-2) Repeat but close 5th *derrière*.

Repeat 4 times in all, keeping movement as smooth as possible. Lower heels, then *relevé* in order to return with left foot leading.

N.B. There is a very slight spring on to the leading foot, but the moment the tips of the toe touch the floor the knee must be stretched. This tiny spring is most important because later when *pas de bourrée courus* are practised the knees must have sufficient flexibility to keep the movement flowing. If they are fully tightened and stretched this is an impossibility.

Rules – Elementary Centre

1 (*Petit adage*) [4/4 in 2 bar phrases.]

Commence in 5th *croisé*.

1. Simultaneously stretch to *pointe tendue devant en fondu*, transfer weight, stretch new supporting leg, close 5th *derrière*. 2 *battements glissés devant* and 2 *glissés derrière*.
2. Repeat in reverse.
3. *Chassé à la 2nde* into *battement glissé à la 2nde*, closing 5th *derrière*, and 2 *glissés* using the other foot. Repeat, moving to other side with other foot.
4. *Grands battements devant* and *derrière* into small 4th *demi-plié* into *pirouette en dehors*, finishing 5th *derrière* in good *demi-plié*. Stretch knees ready to repeat on other side.

Rules – Intermediate *Barre*

9 Stretching at the *barre à la 2nde* to help Turn-out [Waltz.]

Ensure that the supporting leg and foot are placed at a right angle to the *barre* before placing the working leg on top. This means that it will be slightly over-crossed, but hips and shoulders must be parallel and face the same front. With working arm in 2nd, slowly *fondu* and stretch upwards twice on supporting leg, keeping the body and other leg absolutely still. Take working leg off *barre* and correct alignment so that the toe of the working leg is in line with the supporting heel.

Pass that leg through 1st and turning supporting leg slightly inwards (i.e away from the *barre*) place working leg on *barre* in *arabesque*, keeping hips and shoulders as before. *Fondu* twice, then bend body forwards and upwards, arm passing from 2nd to 1st and *arabesque*. Take leg off *barre* and correct both the *arabesque* and alignment. Ensure that hips and shoulder face a correct front with no twist.

Rules – Intermediate Centre

1 (*Petit adage*) [Waltz in 4 bar or 6/8 in 2 bar phrases.]

Commence in 5th *croisé*.

1. *Glissades devant* and *derrière*, full *plié* in 5th, arms 2nd to 5th during descent and through 1st to *bras bas* on ascent. 2 *grands battements devant*.
2. *Grand battement derrière* and *à la 2nde* (these are slow), arms moving 4th to 2nd *arabesque*, close 5th *devant*, *rond en dehors* into 4th *demi-plié* and *pirouette en dehors*, arms 5th, finishing 5th *derrière*, ready to repeat on other side.

Rules – Advanced *Barre*

9 *Battements en cloche* [6/8.]

Commence *pointe tendue derrière*.

These should not be confused with *battements balançoire* (see page 61). In their case the leg swings to and fro, but the body has to be kept as still and upright as possible, except for the stretching upwards and slightly backwards into an *arabesque* line. To perform *en cloche* the dancer needs to feel that the total line drawn from the crown of the head down the fully stretched spine to the pointed toe is swinging to and fro like a pendulum. But on returning from the *arabesque penchée* (see page 4), the head must help to lead the upper torso into a slight curve backwards if the working leg is to rise as high in front as it did at the back.

N.B. No more than 16 should be performed with each leg, and never before the dancer has fully warmed up.

Rules – Advanced Centre

1 (*Petit adage*) [4/4 in a 2 bar phrases.]

Commence in 4th opposite 5th *croisé*.

1. (1-2) Full *plié*. (3) Return to *demi-plié*. (4) Into *pirouette en dehors*, finishing *fondu* into *pointe tendue effacé devant*. (1-and-1-2) Stretch and *fondu*, turning into *pointe tendue écarté devant* and *pas de bourrée dessous*. (3-and-a-4) Repeat stretch and *fondu*, etc. on other side.
2. (1-2-3-4) *Grands battements devant* and *derrière*. (1-2-3-4) Rise making a three quarter turn into *développé devant, tombé en avant* into 4th and *pirouette en dedans* finishing 4th *croisé*, weight on front foot *fondu* (i.e. do not raise supporting heel during *tombé*) straighten knee before repeating whole on other side.

N.B. It is always important to commence with a full *plié* in 4th and to return to *demi-plié* before a *pirouette en dehors*. It is equally important to regain 4th from a *tombé* where the position is larger because the front leg is *en fondu*, ready for a *pirouette en dedans* (usually with a *fouetté*) (see pages 47 and 76).

2 (*Petit adage*) [3/4 in 4 bar phrases.]

Commence in 5th *croisé*.

1. 2 *ronds à terre en dehors* changing *épaulement* to other corner and finishing *pointe tendue derrière*. Pass through 1st to *grand battement devant* and back through 1st to *grand battement derrière*, finishing in 4th *demi-plié*.
2. *Pirouette en dedans* finishing 4th *devant demi-plié* and immediately into another *pirouette en dedans* finishing 5th *devant*.

N.B. These last 2 *pirouettes* should change corners from one to the other. Use *fouetté* movement.

3 (*Grand adage*) *ADAGE* [Slow 3/4 in 2 bar phrases and start on anacrusis.]

Commence *pointe tendue croisé derrière*.

1. (and-a-1) *Pas de bourrée en tournant en dedans* closing 5th and *développé devant* at 90°, arms 1st to open 4th.
2. *Grand rond de jambe en dehors*, arms changing from 4th to 4th and then *arabesque*.
3. *Fondu* into *pas de bourrée dessous* into small 4th *demi-plié*.
4. *Pirouette en dehors* closing 5th *devant demi-plié*, stretch knees ready to repeat on other side.

4 *Pirouettes* as practice for increasing number of turns [4/4 in absolute strict tempo in order to increase the dancer's speed and NOT the musician's. This is essential.]

Repeat as for Ex. **4**, page 64 and repeat 4 times in all to the right, then to the left. Always start by preparing *à la 2nde* and circle to small 4th *demi-plié derrière*, finishing firmly in 5th *derrière*. First perform a single turn, next a double, third time a triple and lastly four – or if impossible, as many as are comfortable and stable.

It is best to repeat all right and then left. If there are left-handed students, then it is valuable to commence to the left. But in all cases practise on both sides.

53 *Temps levé sauté devant,* from *Les Deux Pigeons* (David Peden)

Rules – Intermediate Centre

2 (*Petit adage*) Preparation for *grand rond de jambe renversé* [Slow waltz in 4 bar phrases.]

Commence in 5th *croisé*.

1. 2 *ronds à terre en dehors*, on a third pass through 1st to *attitude devant en fondu*, stretch both legs throwing working leg *à la 2nde* and lowering it to *pointe tendue derrière*, arms move from 3rd to 4th and open 5th. The other arm should be held in 2nd.

2. *Pas de bourrée en tournant en dehors*, finishing 4th; *croisé demi-plié* into *pirouette en dedans*, finishing 5th *devant*; arms pass from 2nd to *bras bas*, 1st and 3rd; ready to repeat on other side.

N.B. The *pas de bourrée* should be danced *en place* as far as possible, girls using *piqué* but the boys a slightly larger step.

3 (*Grand adage*) *Temps lié* [Slow minuet in 4 bar phrases.]

Commence in 5th *croisé*.

1. Simultaneously *fondu* and *retiré devant, bras bas* to 1st; stretch both legs and *développé devant*, arms to open 4th; step straight forwards into 3rd *arabesque fondue* and stretch supporting leg; hold. (Do not pause on *demi-pointe* during the transfer as the body must be seen to rise and sink very smoothly.)

2. *Retiré en fondu*, changing *épaulement* to *de face*; stretch and *développé à la 2nde*, arms to 2nd; step sideways, transferring weight whilst raising other leg *à la 2nde* and slightly bending towards supporting leg, lower whilst lowering arm on supporting side a little; hold before closing 5th *devant* changing *épaulement* ready to repeat on other side.

4 *Pirouettes, pas de bourrée* and *ballonnés* [2/4 in 4 bar phrases. Start on anacrusis.]

Commence *pointe tendue croisé derrière*.

1. (and-a-1) *Pas de bourrée en tournant en dedans* (2-3-4-) *Temps levé* with *ballonné* into small 4th *croisé* (i.e. same side). *Pirouette en dehors*, from 4th to 4th.

2. Repeat this *pirouette* 3 times in all. Stretch to *pointe tendue derrière* and hold, ready to repeat.

N.B. These *pirouettes* must finish and commence from the same *demi-plié*, therefore the placing of the feet must be exact and small and the position held very firmly. The arms must also be controlled and move from 3rd to 1st only. Do not attempt to pass them through *bras bas*.

Rules – Advanced Centre

2 (*Petit adage*) [Tango in 2 bar phrases.]

Commence in 5th *croisé*.

1. *Chassé en avant* to *pointe tendue derrière*, close 5th *derrière* with arms 4th, 2 *battements glissés devant*, arms 2nd.

2. Repeat, moving *en arrière*, arms 4th to 3rd *arabesque*.

3. 4 *ronds en dehors* changing *épaulement* to next corner and finishing *pointe tendue derrière*.

4. Drop heel into *pirouette en dedans* finishing 4th *effacé devant demi-plié* and immediately into *pirouette en dehors* (picking up front foot) finishing 5th *derrière*, ready to repeat on other side.

3 (*Grand adage*) ADAGE [Waltz or minuet in 4 bar phrases.]

Commence *pointe tendue derrière* on the anacrusis).

1. (and-a-1) *Pas de bourrée en tournant en dedans* into (2-3-4) *grand rond de jambe renversé en dehors* and *pas de bourrée en tournant en dehors*, finishing 5th *devant*.

2. Slowly raise leg to 3rd *arabesque*, rotate to *devant* at 90°, drop into small 4th *demi-plié* and *pirouette en dehors*, finishing *attitude croisée*.

3. Stretch into *arabesque fondue*, arms 3rd; *pirouette en dedans* (i.e. use *fouetté*), finishing *attitude croisée*, stretch and *fondu* to *pointe tendue derrière*.

4. *Grand ports de bras*.

4 (*Petit allegro*) [2/4 in 2 bar phrases.]

Commence in 5th *de face*.

1. *Sissonne fermée battue dessus; sissonne fermée battue dessous; entrechat trois derrière; coupé devant* changing *épaulement*.

2. *Chassé, coupé* into *cabriole devant*, close 5th, ready to repeat on other side.

5 (*Petit allegro*) [2/4 in 2 bar phrases and begin on the anacrusis.]

Commence in 5th *de face*.

1. (and-a-1) *Pas de bourrée piqué dessous*. (and-2) 2 *changements*, repeat on other foot.
2. (and-1, and-2) *Echappé* into 4th and close, *échappé* into 2nd and close, changing feet ready to repeat on other side.

6 (*Petit allegro*) *Assemblés divisés* to ensure use of *demi-plié* [Steady 2/4 in 2 bar phrases and begin on anacrusis.]

Commence in 5th *de face*.

1. (and-1) *Demi-plié* into *assemblé dessus*, finishing *demi-plié*. (and-2) Stretch knees and *demi-plié*. Repeat, using other foot.
2. Then 4 *assemblés dessus* without stretching knees between the *assemblés*.

Repeat 4 times in all, then immediately repeat with *assemblés dessous*.

N.B. Ensure that the rules for the head are correctly followed (see page 26). Arms are best held *bras bas* or opening slightly to *demi-seconde* on each slow *assemblé*. Also at this stage the student should remain *de face*, head inclining when going backwards, but using slight *épaulement* when coming forwards, and turning head over the shoulder.

5 (*Petit allegro*) [2/4 in 2 bar phrases.]

Commence in 5th *de face*.

1. 2 *petits jetés derrière*, *petit assemblé derrière*, *grand échappé à la 2nde*, changing feet.
2. Repeat above.
3. *Sissonne ouverte à la 2nde*, *pas de bourrée dessous* and repeat.
4. 3 *entrechats quatre* and one *changement battu*, ready to repeat on other side.

N.B. Keep arms as low as possible, but open sideways to 2nd for *grand échappé* and *demi-bras* for the *sissonnes*.

6 (*Petit allegro*) [2/4 in 4 bar phrases, anticipate first beat.]

Commence in 5th *de face*.

1. (and-1) *Pas de chat* from 5th to 5th. (and-2) *Pas de bourrée dessous*. (and-1-and-2) 2 *brisés dessus*. Repeat on other side.
2. (and-1) *Failli*. (and-2) *Glissade derrière*. (and-3-and-4) *Temps de cuisse*, *sissonne dessous*, *sissonne dessus*, *coupé devant*, *assemblé battu dessous* and 2 *entrechats quatre*, ready to repeat on other side.

5 (*Petit allegro*) [Steady tarantella or 6/8 in 2 bar phrases.]

Commence in 5th *de face*.

1. *Jeté porté à la 2nde*, working leg to *retiré devant*, *ballonné* changing *épaulement* to *effacé* and then *grand jeté en avant*, *assemblé derrière*.
2. *Brisés volés devant* and *derrière*, *assemblé derrière*, *entrechat six*, ready to repeat on other side.

6 (*Grand allegro*) *Temps de poisson* [6/8.]

Commence in 5th *écarté*.

Assemblé battu dessus, arms in *arabesque* line, (front arm up, other down), body in *écarté*; bring arms together *bras bas* and through 1st to 5th spring off both feet turning body slightly to face corner as well as bending it backwards towards fully stretched legs. Feet are therefore held tightly together. Finish in 4th, ready to repeat in series.

N.B. Ensure that the change of *épaulement* is accurate and that the arms, head and body are well controlled. There is a very slight twist from the waist upwards away from the audience, but the head turns towards them so that it is seen behind the raised arms.

As this is usually considered a male step, girls should be encouraged to practise *demi-contretemps* into *assemblé battu dessus* using a similar clear change of *épaulement*, i.e. commencing *pointe tendue croisé derrière* the foot passes through 1st to 4th so that the legs are all but *de face* to a corner, but the arms and body are slightly turned backwards with the head towards the audience and arms in the *arabesque* line. The spring into the *assemblé* must bring the dancer back into the true *écarté* line, the arms usually circling from *arabesque* to *arabesque*, i.e. when in the 4th position the one nearer the audience is slightly higher than the other, but on the *assemblé* they change relationship. The leading arm and head must indicate the height of the jump.

a

b

54   *Tours en l'air* (Anthony Dowson): *a* up into the turn; *b* during the turn. – Compare with photograph 30, particularly for the arms and the head.

7 (*Grand allegro*) *Grands échappés* **[2/4.]**

Commence *de face* in 5th.

2 *échappés fermés* in 2nd, 2 *changements*, and 1 *grand échappé*, i.e. jump up stretching and opening both legs as widely as possible and descend into 5th *demi-plié* having changed feet. The arms should open from *bras bas* through 1st to 5th and 2nd. This helps students to feel the need of co-ordinating arms and legs if height is to be gained. BUT DO NOT ATTEMPT this if there is any instability on landing. This particular way of co-ordinating arms and legs in jumps is a particular feature of English Morris and Scottish Highland dance.

8 (*Grand allegro*) *Grands jetés en avant* **[Tango is valuable and the first step must anticipate the first beat.]**

Commence *pointe tendue effacé devant* and step straight forwards.

2 running steps into *grand jeté en avant* and immediately repeat, commencing with the other foot.

N.B. This *grand jeté* must describe an arc, therefore the weight of the head must be carried from a slightly backward tilt up, over, forwards as the dancer lands in *arabesque*. (See Ex. **9,** page 88).

7 (*Grand allegro*) [Waltz in 4 bar phrases.]

Commence in 5th *croisé* and dance *en diagonale*.

1. Moving upstage: *glissade derrière, assemblé battu derrière, chassé effacé en avant* into *cabriole derrière, passé* to 4th *croisé devant*.
2. *Assemblé derrière* and 2 *sissonnes fermées effacé en avant*, thus changing *épaulement* ready to repeat on other side.

8 (*Grand allegro*) [Strong 2/4 in 2 bar phrases.]

Commence in 5th *de face*.

1. (and-a-1) *Glissade derrière, jeté porté à la 2nde*. (2) *Temps levé* into *attitude croisée* (i.e. change *épaulement*). (and-a-3) Continue turning into 2 running steps and *grand jeté en avant*. (4) *Assemblé derrière*.
2. *Soubresaut, tour en l'air*, (turn towards front foot and change) landing in 5th *devant demi-plié*, stretch knees ready to repeat on other side.

7 *Pirouettes fouettées en tournant* (girls)
8 *Grande pirouette* (boys) [Both danced to a gallop.]

Boys and girls usually commence these *pirouettes* from the same preparation. This gives the necessary impetus for the continuous turn on the supporting leg, which rises and sinks *en fondu* with each turn. Once the boy has established and can hold the working leg *à la 2nde* at 90°, he can concentrate on holding the pelvis and upraised leg firmly fixed and the upper torso and head absolutely centred. However, the girl requires extra impetus to rise from *en fondu* directly *sur la pointe* every time she turns and then, like the boys, to keep herself firmly centred over the supporting leg.

The usual preparation for both boys and girls is from 4th *demi-plié*, although some boys prefer 2nd. Both prepare and so time a double *pirouette en dehors* on the anacrusis that the 1st *fondu* into the *relevé* and opening of the working leg occurs on the first or strong beat of the music.

Girls

Having completed their double *pirouette* they can proceed in two ways;

1. The Italian. Simultaneously with the *fondu* the working leg opens *devant*, circles *à la 2nde* and with the *relevé* whips into *retiré* and turn and so continues to be opened, circled and whipped in with each *fondu* and *relevé*.
2. The Russian. The leg opens *à la 2nde* on the *fondu* and whips into *retiré* with the *relevé* into the turn. This sometimes means that the dancer executes a *petit battement* during the turn in order to maintain turn-out. This is wrong and can lead to loss of equilibrium.

Boys

Having completed their double turn, they sink *en fondu* opening leg *à la 2nde* at 90° and hold it there whilst they continue to *fondu* and rise into another turn *à la 2nde* for as many times as possible (usually a series of 4, 8, 12 or 16) before whipping it back into *retiré* for a final double or triple *pirouette*, usually finishing with a kneel on the floor.

N.B. Both boys and girls must keep firm control over their arms and heads and above all the focus of their eyes. Each time they sink *en fondu*, arms should be in 3rd and immediately open to 2nd and close quickly to 1st for the turn. At no time must either arm move behind or above the shoulder as it is important that both hips and shoulder line should be kept parallel to each other and face the audience momentarily at the beginning of each turn.

9 *Ports de bras* [Waltz in 4 bar phrases.]

Commence in 5th *croisé bras bas*, eyes focusing on the hands.

1. *Fondu* to *pointe tendue devant*, arms to 1st, head inclined to right; transfer weight, arms to 2nd with palms down and turning head to right; raise arms to open 5th; round them to 5th inclining head and body slightly to right.

2. Straighten body and head, arms to 1st; *fondu* sliding *pointe tendue* further backwards and lowering left arm to *bras bas* whilst raising right arm a little higher than 2nd and bending forwards, turn head to right hand; swiftly straighten and turn body towards *pointe tendue derrière*, both arms 2nd and bending slightly backwards over left shoulder.

3. Turn forwards, stretching arms into 4th *arabesque* (i.e. body is now back to audience and head is turned over right shoulder; turn on right foot to come *effacé*, bringing arms to 2nd and bend backwards, head over left shoulder.

4. Straighten right knee and pass left leg through 1st to *pointe tendue devant* raising left arm to 5th (with right still in 2nd), eyes focusing on left hand; open arms to 2nd and close feet 5th, turning and inclining head slightly over right shoulder.

9 *Sauts de basque en diagonale* [2/4.]

Commence *pointe tendue devant*, etc. see page 41).

Step on right foot, simultaneously throwing left leg stretched straight upwards with sufficient impetus to make a complete turn. At the height of the jump the dancer should appear to be thrusting the left leg out in *écarté*. Land on left leg *en fondu*, *retiré* with right foot, ready to repeat movement in a series. The arms should open from 3rd to 2nd and 5th at the height of the jump.

N.B. It is perhaps useful to note that the dancer jumps into *écarté* if moving *en diagonale* as it is easier to 'spot' and make a clear turn 'there and back' – with the eyes, so to speak – with the head. But when moving *en manége*, it is easier to throw the leg upwards so that it appears to be *devant* in the direction travelled. In this way the head can anticipate the next 'spot' in the circle. This is very important if the boy wishes to perform double *sauts de basque*.

9 A *grand ports de bras* [Stately 4/4, slow 6/8, sarabande. Only phrasing is indicated as other music is suitable.]

Commence in 5th *croisé*.

1. Lunge forwards as far as possible into 3rd *arabesque à terre*, ensure that weight is firmly over front foot, back foot fully on floor. There is a straight line from head to toe (i.e. as in *arabesque allongée*).

2. Circle arm to 2nd, turning body away from front foot, but straightening head and turning it over front shoulder.

3. Circle back arm over head, bending body and head over front foot and circling other arm downwards and backwards, i.e. both arms are rounded to appear as part of a circle.

4. Circle back foot to *pointe tendue devant*. Open arms to 2nd and gradually straighten body and head, holding *fondu*.

5. Stretch fully upwards, then bend backwards, head turned and inclined over front shoulder, arms moving from *bras bas* to 1st and 5th.

6. Pass working foot through 1st to *pointe tendue derrière* and transfer weight whilst straightening body and head, and moving arms through 2nd, *bras bas* and 1st. As weight is fully transferred and dancer is *pointe tendue croisé devant*, again bend backwards opening arms to 5th.

7. Straighten body and pivot on supporting leg to *pointe tendue écarté*, holding arms in 5th but turning head over front shoulder. (Dancer is all but back to audience). Continue to pivot to front corner and on reaching *pointe tendue derrière*, open arms to 2nd.

8. Transfer weight *en fondu* to *pointe tendue devant* and bow fully over stretched legs, arms to 3rd before stretching into *arabesque* line. Hold. Then move into the usual *révérence*.

111

PART THREE
Remedial Work

Flat Barre

Barre-work that exercises all the muscles properly and thoroughly but that allows no excessive movement such as stretching, jumps or work *sur les pointes* is known as Flat Barre. This can bring back into working order or keep in tone the muscles of students who have been ill or who have been slightly injured but who do not need complete rest. Such students are unable to dance through a whole class because of lack of stamina or minor pain when they are under pressure but they can be considerably helped by teachers who understand the difficulties and how to overcome them.

It is when setting Flat Barre exercises that the teacher must determine whether the problem has a physical or technical cause. (See Focal Points, pages 5–13.)

After Illness

When a student has returned to class after illness, it is usual to find that muscle tone and control have been lost, particularly in the whole pelvic area, the inner and outer thighs and the ankles. Too long a period of rest in bed can also mean a total loss of balance which creates an inability to centre the weight correctly, even when both feet are on the ground.

After Injury

FOOT AND LOWER LEG

Many small injuries occur because too much stress has been placed on a perfectly turned-out and closed 5th position, or on movements passing through the feet but without the tips of the toes being held fully pointed from the time that the heel leaves the floor until the heel sinks again. This fault and the weight being held too far back on the heel, or the heel not being firmly pressed on the floor after a jump or *relevé*, can lead to inflamed Achilles tendons, sore ankles, and painful first and second metatarsal bones – even to slight stress fractures in the foot or lower leg. A twisted knee may cause rolling or sickling or clenched toes. Badly fitting shoes may cause similar problems.

GROIN OR LOWER BACK

A constant twisting of the hips to increase turn-out can cause injuries to the groin or lower back as can a failure to hold the upper spine away from the waist.

Another cause of lower back pain can be a failure to stretch the lumbar curve as straight as possible together with the extension of the leg backwards in an *arabesque*. This causes an 'arching' of the spine and thus a downwards pressure on the pelvis, which is increased if the student also bends the spine backwards from the waist and not from just below the shoulder-blades.

Such small faults and injuries need to be spotted as early as possible so that even the youngest pupils may learn with the teacher's help to recognise their own problems. Then, as they grow, they will be aware of the consequences if a fault persists.

Procedure

Whatever the cause of the injury or weakness, it is best to concentrate on the Rules and to make sure they are correctly observed. The following points are the same as those which should receive attention in any class during *barre*-work, but they should receive greater emphasis and the focal points be more carefully watched.

a Correct stance is essential at the beginning of each exercise and should be taken in 1st position. (Ex.1, page 26, and Ex.3, page 28.)

b Ensure that the turn-out takes place in the hip-joint and is suitable to the individual. When working with injured students it is better to recommend what is comfortable than to insist on a flat turn-out – particularly if the injury is to groin, knee or ankle. It is more important to see that feet are equally turned out – even with a slight gap between them if there is any risk of further injury from the closing foot to a sore toe-joint, heel or ankle.

c Ensure that the weight is correctly centred between both feet or over one foot, particularly over the injured leg or foot, no matter what degree of turn-out is used or what height the leg is raised.

Encourage students with injuries to any part of the lower leg to practise foot and ankle exercises. The first of these should be done sitting on a chair or on the floor, knees bent, feet flat on the floor. The student draws the metatarsal bones together sideways by all the muscles of the lower foot, without clenching the toes under, but leaving them stretched outwards as far as possible and ensuring the heel remains on the floor.

A second exercise is for the student to sit on the floor, legs stretched to the front. Now raise and stretch the feet upwards and downwards only from the ankle, ensure that they work at right angles to the centre of the legs, which can be turned in or out. Similarly sitting, rotate the feet at the ankle both *en dehors* and *en dedans* always commencing and finishing with fully stretched knees.

Another exercise much used in my early training is to sit on a chair, one leg crossed over the other knee, toes and instep stretched downwards in a straight line. Then hold that leg just below the calf with one hand and with the other slowly press the foot downwards to increase the length and rounding of the instep. This form of self-massage is far more benficial than sitting with feet and toes pressed under a radiator – a current fashion!

d Never allow the working leg to rise higher than 45° from the floor until such time as the muscles are able to hold the position firmly at that height. If the student is naturally loose that flexibility will return when the muscles are ready.

e Ensure that any change of weight takes place through the centre. It is most valuable to change weight frequently from one leg to the other through one of the five positions. This ensures that the muscles on the injured side take equal responsibility and are helped to return to normal working. For example: when practising *ronds de jambe* at the *barre*, I usually make students use *ronds en dehors* with the right leg finishing *détournée* and repeat with the left leg before practising *en dedans*. Another excellent exercise is *battements fondus* using a *coupé* between each stretch so that the weight momentarily rests on both feet between each *fondu*.

f Ensure that the hips and shoulders face the same plane and are parallel to each other and the floor. NEVER allow the upper body to sink or twist at the waist line. Children tire quickly if exercises are too long or the body is held still after injury or illness. I have found it beneficial to introduce a few bars of *ports de bras* and bends of the body during exercises at the *barre*. (See *ports de bras*, page 40.)

g Ensure that the head moves freely at all times. This is very important if the student has to work with both hands on the *barre*.

h Throughout Flat Barre there should be no rises or *relevés* until pain has completely subsided. Also use *demi-* or full *pliés* only to such depth comfortable to the individual. This is most important if the injury is to the knee, Achilles tendon or ankle. On no account allow the heel to leave the floor in *demi-plié* or *fondu*. It must be firmly anchored with the knee directly over the toes and under the hip. If there has been acute inflammation it is advisable to allow the student to wear character shoes. But these must have a flat and not a waisted heel.

i NEVER allow stretching exercises except those given in Floor Exercises (page 119), until the student returns to full class.

j If Flat Barre is given because of an injured knee (i.e. suspected cartilage trouble), ankle or groin, see that the weight is held well forwards so that the student can just 'bounce' lightly up and down in 1st position. This is little more than a brief raising and lowering of the heels. It ensures that all the leg muscles are taking responsibility for the movement. In cases of an injured knee it is also important NOT to use any movement to the back or travelling backwards until pain has disappeared so that there is no danger of the student pressing on the big toe, which can only aggravate the trouble. In addition, insist that the toes of that foot

are not clenched. This requires very careful and sympathetic encouragement.

k Ensure that the supporting leg, even if injured, NEVER moves out of the perpendicular even in *fondu*, even if that injured knee has not yet regained full flexion. Such injured students always show a great reluctance to bend the bad knee. Once activity is allowed, this is one of the first things to be encouraged.

The Exercises

1 *Pliés* [Slow 3/4.]

Both hands on *barre*.

Commence with exercise for correct Stance into *plié* (Ex.2 a and b, page 28) once only and follow with 2 slow *demi-pliés* in 1st turning the head to the right and then left; right *pointe tendue à la 2nde* and repeat 2 *demi-pliés*, and head movement. Right *pointe tendue* closing 3rd and 5th and repeat. If this is not possible, repeat *demi-pliés* in 1st and 2nd.

N.B. As soon as possible increase the mobility of the legs by using 2 *demi-pliés* and 1 full *plié* allowing the heels to rise from the floor even if the *plié* does not reach its full depth.

Do not use 4th opposite 1st or 5th until the above are smooth, without strain and apparently at their greatest depth. 4th opposite 1st or 5th should be avoided until the pain has subsided, if there is any suspected cartilage trouble.

On no account allow an injured student of this kind to force the bend of the knees in *pliés*. It is far more important to see that the muscles stretch upwards on the ascent than that the heels leave the floor with a jerk during the descent. It is not fully realised that whereas when standing correctly the weight is distributed throughout the bones of the legs, in *plié* it is only balanced over the bones of feet and ankles. Therefore when the muscles are holding these much smaller bones in place, they must not be strained in any way.

2a *Battements tendus* [2/4 or 3/4.]

Commence in 1st as turned out as possible and comfortable.

    1. Right *pointe tendue devant*.

    2. Turn fully stretched leg inwards from hip-joint only.

    3. Turn leg outwards.

    4. Close 1st.

Repeat alternate legs twice. Then repeat *à la 2nde* and *derrière* (if comfortable) and *à la 2nde*.

or

2b *Battements tendus* [Slow 4/4.]

    1. Right *pointe tendue devant*.

    2. Turn foot upwards from ankle keeping knee fully stretched and at same height.

    3. Return to *pointe tendue*.

    4. Close 1st.

Repeat using alternate feet four times in all. Then *à la 2nde* and *derrière*. If there is NO knee trouble repeat closing each time in *demi-plié*.

3a *Battements glissés* [2/4.]

Commence in 1st position.

    2 *battements glissés devant* closing second in *demi-plié*. Stretch supporting leg and slowly *retiré*, close 1st.

Repeat with left foot. Then repeat *en croix*. Repeat twice in all.

N.B. The working foot must keep contact with the floor as long as possible, the tips of the toes finally leaving it fully stretched. The working leg must not rise higher than 20°.

or

3b *Battements glissés* [2/4.]

Commence in 1st position.

    1. 2 *battements glissés devant*, closing 2nd in *demi-plié*.

    2. Stretch knees.

Repeat with other foot. Then repeat *en croix*. Repeat twice in all.

N.B. See note for **3a**.

4a *Ronds de jambe à terre* [3/4.]

Commence in 1st position.

    1. *Pointe tendue devant*, circle *à côté* and *derrière* (if possible) close 1st.

    2. Repeat other foot.

    3 – 4. Repeat with supporting leg *fondu* (if possible – if not, with straight supporting leg.

    5 – 6. 4 *ronds en dehors* then repeat with other leg.

    7 – 8. Take hands off *barre* and circle arms by opening them from 1st to 2nd, 5th and return to the *barre*.

Repeat, moving *en dedans*.

or

4b [Very strong 3/4.]

Commence in 1st and use quarter *ronds* keeping the movement very smooth but pressing the heels on floor when closing in 1st.

    1. *Pointe tendue devant*.

    2. Circle *à la 2nde*.

    3. Close 1st.

Repeat other foot. Repeat moving from side to back and 1st. Repeat with other foot. Now repeat whole moving *en dedans*, i.e. back – side, side – front.

N.B. As strength returns repeat more slowly using *fondu*, i.e. simultaneously *fondu* and *pointe tendue devant*, circle *à la 2nde* holding *fondu*, then straighten supporting leg as the other closes in 1st. Continue as above.

    This exercise has proved very valuable for those with any knee troubles. But only use quarter *ronds en dehors* and *en dedans* to front and side until knee has strengthened and there is no pain.

5 *Grands battements* [4/4.]

Commence in 1st and take no higher than 45° and to the front and side only. Accent should be up on the beat.

Repeat eight times with alternate legs, followed by 8 *retirés* with alternate legs, lifting the knee as high as possible, but keeping toe close to the supporting leg.

N.B. Do not use *grands battements devant* if the student is unable to take one hand off the *barre*. And do not use *derrière* until the student is fully stabilised over the supporting leg. Do not use *arabesque* if there is back or groin injury until pain has subsided.

6a *Battements frappés* [4/4.]

Prepare *sur le cou de pied*.

This is not a true *frappé* but a mere swinging outwards and inwards from the knee only, the tips of the toes just brushing the floor. Movement must be very smooth with no jerking of the knee.

3 *frappés à la 2nde*; *fondu* on the third movement inwards, bringing working leg and foot into 1st and *coupé* ready to repeat swing with the other leg.

Repeat four times in all with alternate feet.

or

6b *Battements frappés* [4/4.]

Prepare *sur le cou de pied*.

3 *frappés devant*, the third *en fondu* on the outward movement, circling working leg *à la 2nde* and simultaneously stretching the supporting leg.

Repeat circling *derrière* and then in reverse. Repeat four times in all and ensure the hips do not twist.

7a *Petits battements sur le cou de pied* [2/4.]

Prepare *sur le cou de pied*.

(and-1) Beat *derrière* – *devant*. (and-2) Repeat.
1. Close 3rd or 5th *demi-plié*.
2. Simultaneously stretch supporting leg and *retiré passé derrière* to *sur le cou de pied*.

Repeat in reverse. Then repeat whole.

N.B. Ensure that working foot bends and stretches upwards or downwards at the ankle only, particularly if the injury has been to the ankle.

or

7b Prepare as above and use 3 *petits battements* closing *sur le cou de pied en fondu*, *coupé* and repeat, starting at the back with the other foot.

N.B. In this version ensure the feet change places immediately on the *coupé*, as accuracy is essential to make the injured foot work. It is also essential that the change of weight is swift and directly through 3rd or 5th.

8a *Battements fondus* [6/8.]

Prepare *sur le cou de pied*, or 5th.

1 – 3. Simultaneously *fondu* and bend working leg so that pointed toe rests just above supporting ankle bone.

4 – 6. Stretch both knees equally and simultaneously as working leg moves to *pointe tendue devant à terre*.

Repeat *fondu* and opening *en croix*. After final *à la 2nde*, close working foot in 3rd or 5th.

Repeat with other leg. Then repeat whole, raising working toe to bottom of calf *en fondu* and stretching to 45°. No higher as the movement must be equalised on both legs.

or

8b Commence as above but change weight after each movement, i.e. bring working foot into 3rd with *coupé* so that the legs work successively *devant*, *derrière* and *à la 2nde*. When performed at the *barre* with one hand only, the three *battements fondus* should be followed by *détourné* to repeat other side.

Repeat raising legs to 45°. Repeat twice in all.

9a *Développés* [6/8.]

It is important to commence 3rd or 5th so that the change of weight and its centring over the supporting leg is minimal when performed *en croix* at 45°,

i.e. 1 – 2 – 3. *Retiré*, raise working toe to bottom of supporting calf. 4 – 5 – 6. Raise knee a little, opening and stretching leg outwards at 45°.

1 – 2 – 3. Hold. 4 – 5 – 6. Close.

Repeat *à la 2nde* and *derrière*. *Demi-plié* or simple *ports de bras*.

Repeat with other foot. Then repeat commencing *derrière*.

N.B. Ensure that supporting leg remains perpendicular throughout. But see that the upper torso and head stretch and curve slightly backwards towards the centre when moving into *arabesque*. It is for this reason that *ports de bras* are a better ending than *demi-plié*. (See notes below on *ports de bras*.)

or

9b *Demi-ronds de jambe en dehors* [Slow 3/4.]

Commence 3rd or 5th.

Slowly raise fully stretched working leg to 45° and circle *à la 2nde* closing 3rd or 5th. Continue *en croix*. Move only in quarter circles. Repeat twice with each leg. Then repeat *en dedans*.

N.B. This exercise can also be repeated later from *développés*, but the lifting of the straight leg helps students to gain strength more quickly.

10 Body stretching and *ports de bras* [Very slow 3/4 or 6/8.]

To be used with all injuries except the back, shoulders and groin (if severe) when the degree of bend will depend upon the student's own ability to move without pain. In each case the bend must come only from above the waist, shoulders kept flat, arms and hands pressed slightly sideways and away from each other as they rest on the *barre*.

Commence in 1st.

1. Breathe in and, stretching upwards as far as possible, bend forwards commencing with the head, following with the neck and from just above the waist. Do not allow the shoulders to move. Recover and repeat.

2. Raise one arm through 2nd to 5th, breathe in lifting upper torso from the waist and bend sideways without moving arm or shoulder, i.e. only the body must be seen to bend slightly helped by an inclination of the head. Recover and repeat, changing arms and bending to the other side.

3. Breathe in and turning head slightly to the right, bend backwards without raising the shoulders. Head must lead the movement so that the upper spine can be felt to stretch upwards and over before backwards. After recovering, repeat to the other side. NEVER allow the head to drop straight backwards, most particularly if there has been any injury to arm or shoulder. The head must be slightly on one or the other side during a back bend if any injury is present.

4. (The last phrase of the music.) Bend body slightly to the right, circle it forwards and round to the other side. Straighten and repeat circling the other way.

N.B. Once the dancer is stable and can hold the *barre* with one hand the same *ports de bras* should be given with the exercises. However, he or she should be encouraged to use 3rd or 5th positions and sink as deeply as possible into full *pliés*, to which should be added 4th opposite 1st. Then, if the injury is only minor to any part of the lower leg, introduce slow rises through $\frac{1}{4}$, $\frac{1}{2}$ and $\frac{3}{4}$ *pointes* in 1st, 2nd and 5th positions, ensuring that the weight is taken equally over both legs.

Later introduce rises to *demi-pointe* on the supporting leg in exercises **3b**, **4b**, **7**, **8a** and **8b**. Later introduce a rise to *demi-pointe* whenever lifting the working leg to *retiré* in **3b** and **7**; when closing the feet in 1st in **4b** and on drawing both feet together in **8a** and **b**.

As soon as the dancer gains confidence, give two or three simple *enchaînements* in the centre, utilising exercises practised at the *barre* and *ports de bras*. No *adage* or jumps should be attempted until the legs can rise to 90° at the *barre* and slow rises can be attempted in the centre.

Small jumps should first be introduced at the *barre* in 1st and 2nd positions. These are little more than 'bounces' up and down, but just sufficiently high to allow the toes to be fully pointed. Exercise **6** should allow a slight spring into the *coupé* before attempts are made to jump off one foot. *Temps levés* are particularly important, but very difficult if the injury is to any part of the lower leg. Therefore it should first be introduced at the *barre*. Once *temps levés* have been tried then it is useful to work from 3rd or 5th with one *soubresaut* followed by a *temps levé* lifting the working leg either to the side or behind the other leg, followed by *petit assemblé* in 3rd or 5th *devant* and held in *demi-plié*. Repeat using the other leg and ensure that the landing is equally placed over both feet.

Once such simple exercises have been mastered the student should return gradually to full class, leaving all *grand allegro* steps and *pointe* work as the last items to be attempted.

Floor Exercises

When the dancer is for some time out of practice because of serious illness, a broken limb or an operation to knee, ankle or foot but has begun to exercise under a physiotherapist or on the instructions of an orthopaedic surgeon, it is most valuable – particularly for a dancer aiming at a professional career – to begin to exercise all those muscles that will ensure the regaining of correct Stance, Turn-out and Placing. For it is the muscles in the inner and outer thighs, buttocks, lower spine and stomach which waste and lose tone. As soon as the patient can move, but is not able to take weight fully on the injured limb, or too weak to sustain carriage, it is essential to tone up all the muscles that activate legs and lower spine.

However, Flat Barre should NOT be attempted at this stage. Rather should the dancer lie flat on the floor, legs unturned out, with feet flat and resting lightly on a wall or board. The body must be correctly centred over the legs, shoulders relaxed and pulled downwards, arms spread slightly sideways and on the floor. The 'tail' must be pulled down so that the spine is as flat as possible.

N.B. When the exercises are performed after damage or operation to a knee, they should first be practised without any bending of the knees for two or three days (see page 115). Then a slight bend must be introduced and increased as the knee gets mobile.

Although most of the following exercises should be practised lying on the floor, only three or four should be attempted before allowing the dancer to sit up very straight, with legs resting in front of the body as relaxed as possible, and to perform simple *ports de bras*. (See page 118.) It is sometimes valuable to place a rolled-up towel under the knees.

If, however, a knee or groin gives pain, it is possible to perform the *ports de bras* sitting on a chair. In this case the spine must be pulled upwards as straight as possible so that there is a right angle between the upper thigh and body. With some dancers this may mean that the body has to be brought slightly forwards; with unturned-out legs, both knees should be bent as far as is comfortable, the feet slightly apart, pressed gently on the floor.

Exercises for the Legs

All the following remedial floor exercises have also proved useful to improve and/or correct Stance, Turn-out and Placing and should be practised in addition to the *barre*-work of ordinary classes based on those Principles. The exercises are particularly useful for growing children who are not always able to feel how all their muscles work. This is usually because they strain to be as technically accurate as possible whilst contending with lengthening and broadening bones and shape. The fact that the feet must be pressed against a wall or board helps them to realise the need to press into and out of the floor at the same time as being helped to keep the spine and hips as still as possible. It also helps them to preserve their sense of balance and realise the need always to centre the weight over one or both feet as well as the need to keep the supporting leg (or legs) firmly placed and still.

1 Lying flat on the floor, absolutely straight, legs unturned out, turn both legs slowly outwards and inwards from the hip-joints by drawing all the inner thigh muscles together without raising the spine from the floor. Ensure that the feet remain flat and lightly pressed on the wall. There must be no movement of the pelvis. This can also be practised at a later stage sitting very straight, preferably back against a wall with hands pressed lightly on the floor just in front of the hips, or on the front of the thighs.

A valuable alternative to the above finds the student lying flat, legs turned out, feet against a wall in 1st. Gradually point the feet, opening the legs outwards (toes held on the wall) and stretch them out sideways fully, before closing them again. Care must be taken to see that the hips do not twist in any way in an effort to increase turn-out. Both legs should be equally stretched and toes held on the wall throughout.

Once the above is mastered a bending of the knees should be introduced. Open the fully turned-out legs as above, bend knees, turn bent legs inwards, then outwards, fully stretch legs and close.

Do not practise all the above in the same session, two only are enough and each performed four to eight times according to the severity of the injury.

2 The following exercise and its variation should only be used when the knee is all but fully mobile and there are no pains in the groin or lower back.

With unturned-out legs, toes fully pointed, draw knees upwards as far as possible, toes firmly on the floor and heels drawn together. Allow knees to fall open and, keeping toes stretched and heels as far as possible together, stretch till the toes touch the wall and then flatten the feet. This exercise is particularly useful for those with sway-back legs.

An alternative exercise is to lie with turned-out legs but unpointed toes in what can be called 1st position. Draw the knees upwards, keeping the heels together (as if in *demi-plié*) until they are bent as far as possible. Then stretch legs straight downwards until they touch the wall. There should be no tension felt anywhere when the knees are bent. Do not force them on to the floor. Ensure that the inner thigh and buttock muscles maintain the turn-out and the back is flat without twisting the hips.

This last can also be tried in 2nd position; in this case ensure that a proper right angle is maintained between the upper and lower legs when the knees are fully drawn upwards. Only practise one of these exercises in a session and repeat four to eight times.

3 *Battements tendus* should be practised lying flat as above, legs turned out in 1st. Slowly stretch the right leg upwards to *pointe tendue* by gradually unfolding ankle, foot and toes in proper order so that the toes are never clenched and never all leave the wall. Return to 1st, ensuring that the toes and foot relax in that same order. Repeat with the left leg and then up to eight times with each before repeating all moving to the side. It is also important to ensure that each leg stretches to the same height or width on the wall. If it does not, then care should be taken to see whether one leg is shorter than the other. If it is, it may be possible to encourage the shorter leg to stretch further. If the legs are of equal length then the fault must lie elsewhere and should if possible be found.

4 *Battements glissés* should be practised as *tendus* above, the working foot allowed just to leave the wall. The toes must return to the wall at the same point at which they left it. Also ensure that both legs reach the same height or width without the pelvis twisting in any way.

At a later stage it is valuable to place the legs in 5th position ensuring that the body is correctly centred. Perform 3 *glissés* closing 5th and a fourth closing 1st, seeing that the supposed supporting leg slides outwards sufficiently to allow the working leg to close properly in 1st again with the body correctly centred. This tiny movement helps children in particular to understand the slight change of weight needed when moving from 1st to 5th. The movement should also be practised to the side. In both cases it must be practised slowly without any twisting of the hips. So do NOT allow the working leg to hit the floor when moving to the side.

It is also very useful to practise both *battements tendus* and *glissés* commencing with a small *développé devant* or *à la 2nde* closing 1st or 5th. The foot should be fully stretched as the knee is drawn upwards until the tips of the toes reach just above the ankle bone. At this point the leg should be fully stretched forwards or sideways until the tips of the toes touch the wall. The foot must then be brought back into position without the knee bending in any way or deviating from the turn-out.

5 *Ronds de jambe* are practised lying flat as above. Stretch right leg upwards to *pointe tendue devant*, circle *à la 2nde* and close 1st. Ensure that the tips of the toes never leave the wall and, when repeating with the left leg, ensure that the quarter circle is made exactly the same size as with the right leg. This helps children to understand how to stretch outwards from the hip only and how to use the inner thigh muscles correctly. Repeat 4 times with each leg and then repeat *en dedans*.

It is essential that the turn-out is maintained and the working leg is fully stretched whilst the back remains flat with hips and shoulders level. There must be no twisting of the hips to increase turn-out.

When the above is mastered the *rond* should be practised using an open *attitude devant*, i.e. lift the leg in an open *retireé* as turned out as possible, toe roughly opposite supporting heel and just above that ankle bone. Circle to the side (do not attempt to touch the floor, but use what turn-out is possible) without changing height or angle of leg, then stretch lower leg outwards until toe touches the wall, close in 1st. Repeat four times with each leg and *en dedans*. The *attitude* must be no higher than 45°.

Later *grands ronds de jambe* should be practised in the same way. But no attempt should be made at height, only control of the line. Also, as in the above, no attempt should be made to rest the working leg on the floor when *à la 2nde*. The hips must be kept flat and equally turned out and balanced, for if the pelvis twists in any way the purpose of the exercise is lost. Also ensure that the so-called supporting leg does not move out of the perpendicular.

6 *Grands battements* are best practised in the same way as *glissés*, but the legs will not usually rise as high as when standing because not enough impetus can be given by the push out off the floor, which requires the weight of the leg behind it. Nevertheless it is essential that both working and supporting legs are fully stretched and as turned out as possible. Moreover the supporting leg and hips as well as shoulders must not move in any way. The working leg rarely touches the floor when moving *à la 2nde*.

7 *Développés* should be first practised lying flat, legs unturned out. Raise the right knee upwards with toe unpointed, foot flat on floor; raise knee further, simultaneously pointing toe and turning leg outwards before fully stretching leg *à la 2nde*. Close leg in 1st, keeping it turned out. Repeat with left leg. Repeat opening *devant*, taking care to maintain the turn-out achieved when the knee opens.

N.B The extra lift of the upper leg and slight opening of the knee determines the height of the fully stretched leg. (Page 13.)

It is essential for the student to feel the rotation of the leg in its socket as the leg is stretched outwards by the lengthening of the muscles at the back of the thigh. At the same time the inner and outer muscles are drawn inwards and round with the turn out.

The exercise should also be practised with the legs turned out at the beginning. In this case the knee should be raised, the foot gradually stretching up the side of the supporting leg until the toe reaches at least the middle of the calf. At this point, open the leg slightly whilst raising the knee and go on stretching the leg sideways or forwards, leading the movement with the toe and maintaining the height indicated by the angle of the upper leg.

8   The above exercise can also be practised as a *battement relevé* (or a very slow *grand battement*). The leg is raised upwards, turned in with the toe unpointed and, at the height of the lift, turned out at the hip as the toe is pointed before being lowered.

Help is usually needed in this and in **6** and **7** when first attempted. It is best given if the teacher kneels at the dancer's head and firmly but very lightly places both hands on the sides of the dancer's hips in order to keep them firm. This prevents over-turning, which usually occurs if the feet sickle outwards as they are pointed.

9   Sitting on the floor, back straight against the wall, legs unturned out, draw knees upwards as far as possible, allow them to fall outwards keeping the feet pointed, then stretch both downwards into 1st until fully stretched. Do not allow the feet to sickle. Do not use for anyone with back or groin injury until he is nearly ready to return to Flat Barre.

10   Sitting as in **9** above but away from the wall, breathe in and curve, whole body forwards in proper order, viz. head, neck, shoulders, above the waist and a little below keeping the shoulder flat. Now keeping the toes pointed and knees straight, stretch the spine further forwards and then upwards to flatten it. The arms should curve over the head to 5th with the forward bend and open to 2nd when the dancer is sitting absolutely straight. Once the upright spine is fully stretched with arms in 2nd, and not behind the shoulder, breathe in and bend backwards, i.e. stretch upwards with the head and only then curve backwards from just below the shoulder blades.

This can also be practised arms opening to 2nd during the curve forwards, then drawn into 5th (shoulders down) and held there during the back bend. In either *port de bras* do not allow the lower back to sink into the floor. And on no account allow the arms to go behind the shoulders in 2nd or 5th. Teachers should also ensure that the lower back is as upright and fully stretched as possible. It sould be at right angles to the floor and to the upper legs.

Exercises for Strengthening the Spine

The following exercises are particularly useful in strengthening the spine and muscular corset. They should only be used when the dancer is fully recovered from any injury to knee, groin or back.

1   Lie flat on the floor, arms stretched outwards in *demi-bras*, legs unturned out. Lift and lower legs slowly four to eight times. Then repeat the movement, lifting and lowering the upper torso, having lifted the arms forwards in front of the shoulders, which should be kept as firmly pressed outwards and downwards as possible.

2   Lie flat on the stomach, arms folded under the chin, legs unturned out. Lift and lower the legs slowly from four to eight times without allowing them to part and feeling that they are being pulled downwards and away from the hip-joints. Now switch the movement to the upper half of the body with arms stretched forwards and keeping the hips and pelvis flat on the floor. The head must play some part by leading the spine outwards and backwards.

3   Now attempt to lift both legs and torso simultaneously four to eight times ensuring that the buttock muscles with those of the inner and outer thighs are being properly drawn inwards or outwards and ensuring that the legs are kept together. There should be a feeling that the legs and body are being pulled away from each other by the outwards stretch of both sets of muscles in opposite directions.

The exercise can also be attempted by lifting alternate leg and arm, i.e. lift right arm and right leg as in 2nd *arabesque*; then repeat, using left arm and right leg as in 1st *arabesque*. This exercise helps to ensure that all the muscles are working correctly and that the hips and shoulders in either *arabesque* are facing the same plane. It is for this reason that students must feel the counter-pull of muscles before curving the spine and head into a true *arabesque* line. It also helps them to understand the need always to be in correct alignment through understanding the exact placing of the limbs in relationship to the body.

4   When students find it difficult to direct their legs into an absolutely straight line through the centre, it is useful to make them lie face down on the floor and encourage them to lift the lower leg straight upwards behind the upper leg without in any way twisting foot or ankle. First the legs should be lifted slowly and alternately, and then together. There must be no turn-out.

5   Similarly lying face down, lift the lower leg straight upwards, then let it fall across the supporting one so that the knee slides outwards on the floor, and from this position stretch the leg outwards and downwards with fully pointed toe before closing it to the other. This is to encourage the feeling necessary in the outer thigh muscles. **1** and **2** should make students feel the inner thigh muscles because they are lying on their backs.

Suitable *ports de bras*

It is during sessions of exercises on the floor that I concentrate on *ports de bras*. It is then possible to ensure that students stretch their arms outwards from their bodies by lifting them from underneath whilst keeping their shoulders down and flat on the rib-cage. It is particularly valuable for growing boys, who more often than not tense and press their shoulders backwards and thus lift their rib-cages too high. They think this will help their turn-out! Thus they use neither stomach nor inner thigh muscles correctly. It is most important to insist that when they sit on the floor or a chair their spine is stretched upwards as far as possible and their shoulder-blades feel flat and down. This feeling is equally important in girls.

1 Sitting upright and using only head and arms, use any *ports de bras* moving through all the usual positions except *bras bas*.

2 Open arms from 1st to 2nd, twist sideways from right to left, keeping head straight and without allowing arms to fall behind the shoulders or straighten. Perform four times and then repeat turning head over arm coming in front. Next time repeat turning head over arm moving behind.

3 Sitting absolutely straight (if on a chair it should be fairly wide), press both hands on the floor by the sides of the upper thighs without raising the shoulders. Then press arms upwards over the head, looking up but without raising shoulders.

4 From 1st position, slightly twist body to the right, moving arms to closed 4th, but turn head over left shoulder. Then reverse the movement. Each time the arms should pass through but never overcross in 1st or closed 4th.

5 As **4**, but press one hand on floor just behind thigh and the other hand and arm straight upwards, head turned across shoulder of upraised arm. Reverse the movement.

In both **4** and **5**, the twist must come from the waist only. The hips must not move.

6 From 1st, move arms to closed 4th and bend exactly sideways. Then reverse arms by moving back to 1st, straightening the body before bending to the other side.

7 For use with anyone having a stiff or weak back. Sit absolutely straight, legs outstretched on the floor (with care this can be attempted if sitting on a chair – but on no account try if the chair tilts in any way). Raise arms to well rounded 5th, breathe in and stretch forwards as far as possible, merely directing the movement with the head and bending as far as possible from the hip-joint only. Shoulders and arms should not move from their relative positions. Many students can all but rest their head on their legs without bending their spines, or only very slightly. Then

122

Notes on Particular Injuries

When students are ready to start 'Flat Barre' after the muscles have been brought back into tone by floor exercises, teachers should consider the particular injury or operation and adapt their exercises to suit the individual. The following general notes present some guide lines.

Injuries to Feet or Toes

viz. Dropped metatarsal arches, suspected hallux valgus, minor stress fractures

Such injuries can be due to badly fitting shoes, particularly if these are too tight and cause the toes to curl upwards, or to be clenched. Injuries can also be caused by undue pressure on the metatarsal arch because of a failure to keep the tips of the toes in contact with the floor as they leave and return to position with the knee fully stretched. The injury can also be caused by incorrect weight bearing, most probably where it is placed too far back on the heel, or by a curling-under of the toes due to a very high instep with its usual weak ankles.

For all such injuries take all the precautions mentioned for Flat Barre (page 114) and work with the student facing the *barre* and with both hands lightly placed on it. Then note the following.

1 Ensure that the injured foot bends and stretches upwards and downwards at a clear right angle to the lower leg, i.e. the centre of the foot must be directly under the centre of the knee. This is vital in all *pliés* and *battements* and any exercise using a full stretch from hip to toe, followed by a placing of the working foot on the floor in an open position.

2 When bringing the working foot back to 1st or 5th position, ensure that the toes begin to relax as the heel is pressed downwards and inwards. There must be a smooth continuous movement. On no account press on the metatarsal arch causing the toes to curl upwards (page 7).

3 Once the fore-foot becomes more flexible and pain-free, encourage full *pliés* in 1st, 2nd, 3rd or 5th unless the student has a large instep or tight Achilles tendon.

---

slowly stretch the spine upwards as the arms open to 2nd. Come only as far as the upright position and if this is stable, attempt the usual back bend turning the head to left or right. Do not bend straight back with the head. Repeat this bending to and fro very slowly and at the most four times.

In these cases it is advisable not to allow the heel to rise higher than *demi-pointe* until such time as there are no painful reactions. It is also important to add rises to quarter *pointe* only in *pointe* exercises when the feet are in one of the above positions. Later the same rise can be encouraged on one foot. Only when this is accomplished is it wise to increase the height of the rise and the depth of the *plié*. Do NOT use 4th until there is no discomfort at all.

4   Avoid all *pirouettes, rotations, voyagés* and long balances on one leg. When it is possible to *pirouette*, it is best to rise using a strong pressure upwards on to *demi-pointe* and not to a *relevé*, although this will be needed later in *pointe*-work. The rise to *demi-pointe* is usual for boys, but is also valuable for girls because it strengthens the ankles.

Injuries to Ankles and Achilles Tendons

These can be due to the over-correction of rolling or sickling feet which has led to the weight being placed too much either on the inner or, more often, on the outer side of the foot. Ensure firstly that the foot is correctly placed on the floor, with unturned-out legs, and insist on a raising and lowering of the heels to quarter and *demi-pointes* until the centring of the weight over the longitudinal and metatarsal arches becomes habitual. This rising and falling will also help to eradicate the fault of pulling the heel back into the Achilles tendon and the over-arching of the instep which can result in the student all but dancing on the toe nails. A fault which can also cause fractures.

1   It is often valuable, particularly in the case of painful Achilles tendons, to insist that the student works in character shoes with low flat heels. The heel allows the student to carry the weight more forwards and thus encourages him or her to feel the full stretch of the leg downwards and away from the hip-joint, because the weight has been adjusted to allow the inner and outer thigh muscles to work harder.

If the ankle is merely strained through over-work or working wrongly, the same remarks apply as those above on the injured Achilles tendon. However, if it is sprained, much greater care and patience are needed. The bruising and swelling must be allowed to subside before any dance movement is attempted. Floor exercises are most valuable in keeping the leg muscles in tone provided that no emphasis is placed on the action of the injured ankle.

2   Take all precautions mentioned in **1** and **2** above for injuries to toes, etc. (page 122) but use only 1st and 2nd positions and quarter or at the most *demi-pliés* and, no matter how small, *fondus*. The heel must on no account leave the floor. It is essential that one or both feet are flat when weight bearing.

3   Until the injured foot gains some mobility it is valuable to give movements to the side only, particularly if there is limited turn-out. Also ensure that the inner and outer thigh muscles work properly, weight central and away from the waist. It is also valuable to use quarter *ronds à terre en dehors* and *en dedans* only (i.e. front, side and 1st and in reverse) in a series of four with each foot, the heel pressing down gently in 1st. This helps the legs to work equally and prevents the hips from twisting.

4   A simple unaccented form of *battements frappés* is valuable for ankle and Achilles tendon injuries. Standing firmly on the supporting leg, swing the working one outwards and downwards, and inwards and upwards sideways from just above *sur le cou de pied* at such an angle that the metatarsal arch strokes the floor, so to speak, before the foot is fully pointed and strokes it back on return. (It is said to 'suck' the floor.) Repeat this four times before changing feet. Do not accent the movement in any way.

It is also valuable when dealing with any injury to the lower leg, once the ankle, foot and toes are fairly mobile, to practise *flic-flac* without turning (see Intermediate **6** page 59). But ensure that the foot and lower leg alone do the work. Practise first without a rise on the first inward movement, but as soon as some confidence is restored in the injured part's ability to move, add a rise as the foot 'flicks' in and hold it during the 'flac', lowering *en fondu* as the working leg stretches to *pointe tendue*.

It is also useful to practise *petits battements* somewhat similarly. Commencing *sur le cou de pied*, foot firmly pointed, but bent appropriately and placed over the ankle bone, brush the tips of the toes outwards and inwards so that they all but or do touch the floor through the whole movement.

All three exercises help the flexibility of the ankle, arches and toes provided that the foot is seen to move upwards and downwards only at right angles to the lower leg and centre of the knee.

Injuries to Knee
Particularly cartilage trouble or misplaced knee-cap with or without an operation

There are many reasons for these injuries, probably first amongst them being fast growth in children without enough attention being paid to the pressure on the knee-cap caused by over-turning out the feet. This happens because turn-out is not happening in the hip-joint but in the knee, or even possibly the ankle. The first thing is to assess the degree of turn-out available from the hip. If it is poor, then after a period of floor exercises (at least twelve sessions if the injury is serious), whatever degree of turn-out there is naturally should be used until confidence is restored. The student must be able to feel that the leg will take the weight and hold it.

Other causes of knee trouble are the usual ones of erratic growth, particularly when it is fast and when there are such natural physical anomalies as the knee and foot not facing the same direction, i.e. if the leg turns out from the hip, but the knee-cap still faces front, or the foot is set at a different angle not directly under the knee. Floor exercises for turn-out can help these cases, but not always.

No matter what the cause, no dance movements of any kind should be attempted until the orthopaedic surgeon or physiotherapist in charge advises such a course. Floor exercises must always be the first consideration. These must take a slightly different form.

a The feet should rest only very lightly on the wall and never press it.

b Most exercises should first be practised with straight legs. Those entailing the fully stretched legs being turned in and out from the hip-joint are very strengthening as they activate all the muscles in the upper legs, pelvis, buttocks and stomach as well as helping the student to feel the straight line of the spine.

c *Ports de bras* should be practised sitting upright, both legs unturned out, bent equally and slightly apart, feet flat to the floor. Do NOT practise *ports de bras* sitting on the floor.

Once the student can take weight, work should begin facing the *barre*, holding it with both hands. Then take the following precautions:

1 Before attempting any *plié*, test stance by using Ex.1 (page 26) and the depth and degree of *demi-plié* (Ex.2 page 26) but only use what is possible, which may be very little.

2 Work in 1st and 2nd positions only and use NO movements to the back. This will prevent any pressure being placed on the big toe in order to appear more turned out. Very often after an injury or operation to the knee, particularly the removal of a cartilage, students do not immediately regain their feeling of correct Stance, nor of stretching all the necessary muscles to counter-balance each other. Thus they usually fail to adjust their weight correctly, particularly when the injured leg is supporting. They often tend either to arch their spine, or allow the weight to sink on the good leg, in order to protect the injured knee.

3 With most such injuries it is valuable continually to change weight and particularly so when the knee is the problem. The weight should be transferred carefully through 1st, 2nd and later 3rd or 5th positions. The 3rd should be introduced fairly early as it helps to keep the body more fully centred (over both legs or one) and also prevents a too vigorous closing together of the feet. Vigorous closing does produce an uncomfortable feeling that the injured leg is giving way – a feeling that must be always avoided.

4 When first leaving the *barre* it is best to practise simple *pas marchés en avant* only (Ex.1 page 34) ensuring that the step falls through the whole foot and that both feet are carefully joined. Attempt the two rises to quarter *pointes* only. The degree of turn-out is immaterial, but the equal balance on both feet is all important.

5 As soon as the student gains confidence in the knee's ability to work correctly it is valuable to concentrate on *battements fondus à terre* with a transfer of weight between the *battements* and with movement to front and side only. Then repeat, changing weight through quarter *pointes* (Ex.8 page 86).

6 It is difficult to calculate how long it will take for this type of injured student to get back to normal 'Flat Barre' and to work with the leg *derrière*. I usually manage to persuade such students to try *demi-pliés* after six sessions (a week's work) and a first *tendu derrière* about the same time. But it usually takes at least eighteen sessions before they are fit to pretend to jump. Then it is only a matter of encouraging them to 'bounce' up and down by relaxing their legs into *demi-plié* and then stretching them right upwards until their toes are about to leave the floor. But ensure that the heels press into then out of the floor and that all the upper thigh muscles are working and drawn together at the height of the jump.

7 As soon as the student feels able to jump at all, *petits jetés* using the soft *frappés* mentioned above should be tried (page 123). The working leg brushes out from *sur le cou de pied* and then slightly springs back to sink *en fondu* as the other brushes out. It is only when the *petits jetés* can be managed that any attempt at *temps levé* should be tried. But if the weight is fully centred over the foot, as it should be in the *jetés* and not, as so often happens, back on the knee, it can be managed – even if it has to be tried with both hands on the *barre* which can help to lift the body upwards.

8 Eighteen sessions are usually needed before any attempt is made at *pirouettes*. These are best practised first at the *barre*, the dancer rising into *retiré devant*, closing 5th *demi-plié*, then repeating the rise into a half turn, closing 5th *derrière* ready to repeat with the other foot. (Ex.6 page 70). Continue practising until a full turn can be managed and only then try in the centre.

En dedans pirouettes require much confidence as the inner and outer thigh muscles on the injured side require the greatest possible control and strength. When first attempted they must be taken from a small 4th without any *fouetté*. (See page 70.)

9 After five weeks' constant work the student should be able to work through Flat Barre and possibly more normal *barre* exercises and on into the centre for *petit* and *grand adage*, provided that they do not balance too long on one leg. They may be able to tackle single *pirouettes en dehors* and one or two *petit allegro* steps, but NOT *batterie*, where confidence takes longer to return than in anything else. After a week of more or less normal but simple class, students should attempt one *grand allegro* step without any turns in the air. Girls should also take the first steps on *pointes*, but only in well-fitting shoes and at the *barre*.

N.B. The times given are only approximate as knee conditions vary considerably. So do students' temperaments. The teacher's first concern is to make them have confidence in their own ability to control and work the knee correctly. One boy got back to his own class in four weeks after a cartilage removal. Another took nearly three months before achieving a double *pirouette* and a *grand jeté en tournant*. The former grew very slightly before and after the operation. The other was growing fast all the time.

Injury to Groin or Lower Back

Such injuries are firstly, and most usually, the result of an over-turning of the legs either before the muscles are ready or from faulty stance, such as a slight twist inwards on the supporting side to make the working leg appear more turned out. Secondly, they can happen through a 'rocking' instead of a proper 'tilting' of the pelvis in the performance of *arabesques*, a bad landing from a jump, or a faulty back or side bend. Thirdly, they can be caused by the sinking of one side of the torso into the hips. Fourthly, they can be due to incorrect holding of the arms. They are often held too high and/or too far behind the shoulders, or incorrectly rounded by the upper arm being lifted up and forwards in order to round the elbows. This inhibits the spine from working properly, particularly in *arabesques* and back bends because the vertebrae are crunched against each other and the spinal curves can no longer act as shock-absorbers.

1 In all such injuries the vital focal point is the stability of the 'muscular corset'. Ensure firstly that the three points of balance of the feet are firmly placed on the floor and that the inner and outer thigh muscles are used correctly and above all that the weight is correctly centred and held away from the hips.

2 Take all the precautions already mentioned and insist that the turn-out is equal in both legs and appropriate to the individual. See that both feet are set on the floor at the same angle. Allow the legs to rise no higher than 45° in any exercise (20° during the first stages of work) and only use alignment which means that there is no twisting or unevenness in the lines of hip and shoulders. These must lie parallel and facing the same plane. But at the same time insist that the spine remains flexible although no bends of the body should yet be attempted. The body must respond to all transfers of weight. (See page 10.)

3 Whatever is practised the weight must be centrally balanced, particularly when in 5th, when neither foot should be forced to lie flat against the other. It is far

more important with such injuries to concentrate on the carriage of the head – which must be seen to be erect – and over the hips, pelvis and waistline.

4 Do not use 4th opposite 5th until pain has completely subsided and only use 4th opposite 1st after a week's work, and then only when passing through 1st into some other step. If used earlier, the centring of the weight over two, perhaps poorly turned-out, legs can cause problems with the relationship of feet to knees and hips. The latter must be square to a front at all times.

Injury to Head, Neck or Shoulders

Such injuries are comparatively rare and seem to occur more often in boys than girls, and often after problems met in double-work during a period of growth. Cases are very varied. The girl can be too tall when on *pointes*, too short, too heavy or insufficiently aware that both girl and boy must be responsible for correct performance. It is not only the boy that has to take weight. The girl must help. But such injuries can also arise from incorrect use of the head. For example, if the head does not lead the upper torso backwards in a back bend, but stays firmly fixed in place, all the neck muscles tense, the student panics and either jerks the head forwards or lets it fall backwards. This can cause great pain and loss of nerve and, in cases of extreme tension, complete loss of balance. It must always be remembered that the seat of balance lies within the ear. Any tension in the region of head, neck or shoulders can easily upset it.

1 It is essential that the head and/or shoulders and particularly the arms in their sockets move as freely and independently as possible, even though the range may be limited if pain is present. Simple bending, stretching, turning and inclining movements of the head alone should be encouraged. The eyes must be trained to focus directly from one 'spot' to another. For example: as the head turns, the eyes focus on a 'spot' to one side, and then immediately on a 'spot' at the same level on the other side. They SEE nothing in the middle of that line. Similarly the eyes focus on a corner of the ceiling and then on a 'spot' on the floor in the opposite corner. This concentration on the work of the eyes – so useful for *pirouettes* – usually helps the student to regain the mobility of the head, neck and to some extent the shoulders.

Somewhat similar movements of great simplicity should be given to the shoulders as the head moves to indicate direction. They will help to relax tension. Shoulders, too, can be lifted gently up and down, rotated and drawn inwards or pressed outwards together or separately. In addition the student should practise circling the arms from *bras bas* through 1st to 5th and 2nd without allowing the shoulder-blades to move or rise. This can be done by facing a flat wall and merely circling the forefingers up and round on it.

2 To attempt the following *ports de bras*, which I have found of value, ensure that the shoulders are kept level, the shoulder-blades pulled outwards from the rib-cage and held downwards as flat as possible. Use a rounded *demi-seconde* and raise the arms to 2nd and down again before raising them to 5th. And when this has been mastered, proceed to the usual lift from *bras bas* through 1st or 2nd to 5th. But never hold the arms too long in one position, particularly if they have to rise above shoulder level, i.e. in closed or open 4th, closed or open 5th and in certain *arabesques*. Just as weight should be constantly changed by those with leg injuries, so *ports de bras* should be varied continually and the arm on the injured side not be allowed to hang loose. (See pages 8 and 9 to find correct placing of the arms.)

Final Words on Injuries

Teachers should never diagnose. Although not every doctor, orthopaedic surgeon or physiotherapist understands the problems facing dancers, it is their task to diagnose what the injury or pain is. However, unless it is a genuine accident, such as falling over and breaking something, they can rarely tell the *causes* of a particular injury because very few have studied classical dance. Teachers can help in this respect because they have, or should have, trained their own bodies to feel why something is wrong and their eyes to see the fault. The movements of classical dance are infinitely varied and physical make-up and anatomy so individual that dancers cannot always obey the Rules that ought to be followed. Teachers must, as a duty, help students to understand their own physical ability and to keep to the Principles and Rules laid down by the great masters past and present. By so doing they are more likely to produce dancers whose movements give joy not only to themselves, but to all who watch them from the other side of the footlights. (See photo 55.)

55 The Bluebirds finish their *pas de deux*, from *The Sleeping Beauty* (Ravenna Tucker and Phillip Broomhead)